FIFTY YEARS OF
CHINESE PHILOSOPHY

O. BRIÈRE, S.J.

Fifty Years of
Chinese Philosophy

1898 – 1950

TRANSLATED FROM THE FRENCH
BY LAURENCE G. THOMPSON

PREFACE BY E. R. HUGHES

GREENWOOD PRESS, PUBLISHERS
WESTPORT, CONNECTICUT

Library of Congress Cataloging in Publication Data

Brière, O
    Fifty years of Chinese philosophy, 1898-1950.

    Translation of Les courants philosophiques en
Chine depuis 50 ans.
    Reprint of the 1956 ed. published by Allen &
Unwin, London.
    Bibliography: p.
    Includes indexes.
    1. Philosophy, Chinese--20th century.
2. Philosophy, Chinese--Bibliography. I. Title.
[B5231.B713 1979]   181'.11   78-31391
ISBN 0-313-20650-3

181.11
B 853

First published in 1956.
Translated from the original French.

Reprinted with the permission of George Allen & Unwin Ltd.

Reprinted in 1979 by Greenwood Press, Inc.
51 Riverside Avenue, Westport, CT 06880

Printed in the United States of America

10 9 8 7 6 5 4 3 2 1

PREFACE

WHEN I left England for China in 1911, she was still under the rule of the Manchu court. When I arrived, P'u Yi had published his abdication: the Revolution had come. Thus the years of my acquaintance with China correspond pretty much with the time span covered by M. Brière's philosophical bibliography. In 1922 I made my first visit to Peking and there met some of the new intellectual leaders.

The first year of the Republic came to be known as Kwang Fu, which in terms of English metaphor means 'the swing of the pendulum bringing a return of light'. I have always thought that there was a great deal more behind that idea than is to be found in the conventional Western belief that about that time Chinese scholars not only woke up to the values in Western science and institutions but also abandoned their old gods for these new ones. For one thing, there were all those older scholars who recognized the needs of the times, were interested, attracted, and stimulated even by the new studies, but never doubted but what the Great Tradition would hold its own. So also in the radical wing there were men like Professor Ch'ien of the Normal College who changed his name to 'Doubt Antiquity'. Fiercely iconoclastic as some of them were about many of the hoary old beliefs, they were none the less convinced that antiquity had new treasures to disclose under the pressure of sterner critical methods.

That whole movement in China, about and after the turn of the century, is too often regarded as a pretty straightforward affair, a discarding of outworn shibboleths for an obviously more real and vital set of values discovered in Europe and America. Père Brière's list reveals that there was much more to it than that. Alongside of the acclaiming of the new, there existed a profound sense of what in terms of ethics was an act of humility. Men imbued with the pride of scholarship confessed to each other that whereas post-Renaissance Europe had set itself to foster new powers of the mind, their Chinese scholar forebears had busied themselves mainly with intellectual tithe and cummin.

Another thing that comes home to me, as I recall the authors in the list, is the way in which the more specialized philosophers among them reveal the scholar tradition of China. Not that they have waited till they were old before publishing. Some of them have emulated the immortal Wang Pi of the third century by writing notable works in their early twenties. But the strain of perfectionism comes out very clearly in the

5

thinkers who are really respected in thinking circles. One wonders how this spirit will fare under the new political regime. If the authorities decide that it is not unto the edification of the nation as a whole, it surely will be very hard to eradicate.

Dr. Laurence Thompson and his publishers have done a very praiseworthy act in giving Père Brière's diligent cataloguing and appraising the wider public of the English-speaking world. Not only sinologists and librarians will profit from this: anyone who takes the history of ideas seriously will find here much food for thought.

E. R. HUGHES

TRANSLATOR'S FOREWORD

DESPITE an increasing interest in the Occident concerning Chinese philosophy, there is still a dearth of materials on that subject available in Western languages. Among the materials we do possess, a disproportionate amount deals only with the period of antiquity, the 'formative period' of Chinese thought. There are wide gaps in our acquaintance with the whole story, leaving long ages completely blank to the non-Orientalist, and vague enough to the student who reads Chinese. It is odd, but true, that one of the periods on which there is the least material available is our own. And yet it is impossible even to understand the contemporary social and political history of China without knowing of the currents and cross-currents of thought which have been at the bottom of that history.

Hence the importance of the present work, which surveys the philosophical history of China during the first half of the present century. It was originally published in French, in the *Bulletin de l'Université l'Aurore* (Shanghai), série III, tome 10, Octobre 1949, no. 40, pp. 561–650, under the title: 'Les courants philosophiques en Chine depuis 50 ans (1898–1950)'. The following reasons have motivated translation of this article and publication in book form: first, the contents would be of interest not merely to sinologists, but to a wider circle of students of intellectual history in general; second, there are undeniable advantages to having materials in one's own language, even though most students might be presumed to be able to read the original; third, the fact that the article appeared in a journal, and one which is obtainable in very few places outside of China, made it likely that it would become 'buried' for all practical purposes.

The wide range of Father Brière's reading in Chinese philosophical literature, as well as his keenness and objectivity, will be apparent upon examining this work. In no other study has there appeared such a comprehensive bibliography as the author presents here, nor has any previous study covered the period with anything like the thoroughness of this one. The exposition brings out clearly the details of the intellectual ferment and spiritual strife which have underlain social and political events in contemporary China.

Besides the actual translation, the translator has performed the following functions: correction of some typographical errors in the text, supplying

7

of some explanatory footnotes, and appending of a supplementary bibliography of writings in Western languages which also deal with the subject or with certain aspects of it. While adherence to the author's text has been as close as possible, a few liberties have been taken for the sake of a smoother style or clearer presentation. In particular, the translator has assumed responsibility for translation of all titles from the Chinese, since the author was not consistent in his translations, and the reader would therefore have been confused in identification of certain writings. An index has been provided, to which the reader should turn for Chinese characters and dates (wherever it was possible to provide them) of all Chinese mentioned in the text or bibliography. This index also has a section in which are listed all non-Chinese persons mentioned in this work. It was felt that this index would be sufficient for the convenience of the reader, as the work is sufficiently divided into sections that it is easy to find a desired topic by reference to the table of contents.

It will be of interest to note that, as of the date of writing of this Foreword, the following philosophical writers discussed by Father Brière have left the mainland of China rather than remain under the Communist regime, and are now either in Formosa or Hong Kong:

AI Wei—now a member of the Examination Yüan
CH'EN K'ang—professor at National Taiwan University
CH'EN Ta-ch'i—professor at National Taiwan University
CH'IEN Mu—President, Hsin Ya Academy, Hong Kong
FAN Ch'i—professor, Provincial Taiwan Teachers College
FAN Shou-k'ang—professor, National Taiwan University
FANG Tung-mei—professor, National Taiwan University
HUANG Chien-chung—professor, Provincial Taiwan Teachers College
HU Ch'iu-yüan—member, Legislative Yüan
JEN Chüeh-wu—member, Training Committee, Kuomintang Headquarters
LIN Chung-ta—professor, Provincial Taiwan Teachers College
LO Chia-lun—Vice-President, Examination Yüan
T'ANG Chün-i—professor, Hsin Ya Academy, Hong Kong
WANG Shao-lun—professor, Provincial Taiwan Teachers College
WU Chih-hui—in retirement in Formosa
YEH Ch'ing—publisher, Pai Mi Erh Bookstore, Taipei

The following persons have had some share in the carrying out of the present project, and to them the translator wishes to express his sincere thanks:

Fathers O. Brière, S.J., the author, and J. Dehergne, S.J., formerly managing editor of *Bulletin de l'Université l'Aurore*, for kindly permitting translation and republication in the present form.

Dr. Richard A. Gard, formerly with P. D. and Ione Perkins Oriental Bookstore of South Pasadena, California, who originally called attention to the desirability of translating this article.

Prof. Ernest R. Hughes, late Reader in Chinese Philosophy and Religion in Oxford University, who added his recommendation, and made a number of corrections in the manuscript.

Dr. Derk Bodde, Professor of Chinese in the University of Pennsylvania, who went over the manuscript carefully, and made many constructive suggestions.

Miss Irene Tsou 鄒　雲 , of the staff of the United States Information Service of the American Embassy, Taipei, who kindly typed the manuscript.

For the assistance acknowledged above, the translator is indebted, while he of course must assume sole responsibility for the translation in its final form.

LAURENCE G. THOMPSON

Taipei, Formosa
December, 1952

CONTENTS

PART THREE: THE SYSTEMS OF OCCIDENTAL DERIVATION

Fifty Years of
Chinese Philosophy

THE history of Chinese thought during the last centuries was almost entirely dominated by neo-Confucianism. This school of philosophy, the reaction of Confucianism against Taoism and Buddhism, arose during the Sung dynasty, in the eleventh century. Taoism, by its worship of pure 'nature' and its contempt of civilization, and by its theory of *laissez-faire* (which not long since inspired Tolstoy), set itself up as the enemy of all progress. Buddhism, by preaching the 'emptiness' of all things and the escape from this world, had eventually the same result. The philosophies of these two systems, eminently anti-social and unsuitable to the governing of a State, provoked a reaction in favour of Confucianism, an essentially positive system of politics and morals.

The neo-Confucianism of Chu Hsi and Wang Yang-ming

Among the thinkers who were at the head of this intellectual renaissance, two names are outstanding, those of Chu Hsi and Wang Yang-ming. These men represented two very different currents of thought within neo-Confucianism. If Chu Hsi be regarded as the most orthodox interpreter of Confucian thought as adapted to new circumstances, it is not less true that his essentially rationalizing influence led to positivism. Until the last days of the Empire his memory was officially honoured as the equal of the Great Sages of primitive antiquity. On July 17, 1894, a decree of Emperor Kuang Hsü proscribed under the most severe penalties the sale of a book attacking the doctrines of Chu Hsi: 'It is never permitted for anyone to introduce opinions contrary to those of Chu Hsi, something which would do great harm to our literature.'[1] Happily the authority of Chu Hsi was often breached by that of Wang Yang-ming, leader of the idealist school. While Chu Hsi placed the accent on 'things', on the 'exterior sense norm', Wang Yang-ming was devoted to the study of the human heart, of the 'interior sense' of the mind. His moral teaching, which gave the primacy to the life of the mind, exercised a great influence in China, especially in the century which followed his death. In Japan the doctrines of Chinese philosophy were still more durable and had a more profound effect on the intellectual world. At the end of the nineteenth century and in the twentieth century Wang Yang-ming had a renewal of favour in China, perhaps by reaction against the influence of Occidental materialism. Thus one is right in saying that 'the intuitive Confucianism of Wang Yang-ming, which prepared the awakening of Japan, appears to have played the same role in the awakening of China.'[2]

The precursors of modern thought

In the second half of the nineteenth century, the major Chinese scholars were profoundly under the influence of the ideas of Wang Yang-ming. K'ang Yu-wei, the great statesman at the end of the Ch'ing period, was a convinced Confucianist. Believing that the prosperity of the Occidental nations came from their political system and their religion, he wished to make Confucianism a national religion and to attempt a *coup d'état* in order to overthrow the absolute monarchy of the Empress Dowager, Tz'u Hsi, in favour of a constitutional monarchy (1898).[3] The project fell through, and K'ang escaped into exile. In the domain of ideas he is revealed by his *Book of the Universal Concord*.[4] There he asserts that Confucius has divided the course of history into three periods: the stage of disorder, the stage of progressive peace, and the stage of universal peace or great harmony. In the first stage reign egoism, individualism, nationalism, capitalism. In the second stage the nations unite under the aegis of socialism and internationalism. In the third stage humanity will be united in a single civilization. This will be perfect peace. The author describes the conditions of this Utopian fraternity, conditions so audacious and so revolutionary that they were scandalous at the time. Thus, for example, he even went so far as to advocate 'community of women' (*'épouses communes'*)!

After the failure of his attempt in 1898, he lived in exile and, curiously enough, became in a sense a conservative. He became more and more a fervent admirer of Confucius and an obstinate partisan of constitutional monarchy—which is why he was one of the champions of the opposition to 'science' and 'democracy', the two slogans born with the Republic of 1911.

One of his most brilliant disciples and colleagues, T'an Ssu-t'ung, was also a fervent Confucianist. In 1896 he published his *Theory of Jen* (仁 學), wherein he worked out the Confucianist ideal adapted to modern requirements. For him *jen*, that is to say humanity, goodness, kindness, the central virtue of Confucian morals, had a universal penetration like that of ether, electricity, or spirit. When this virtue of *jen* shall be realized on earth, the perfect unity of the world will be assured. Then all the distinctions and inequalities of nations, of classes, and of sexes will be abolished. So it is necessary to put this moral philosophy into practice for the welfare of the universe. This attempt to synthesize Confucianism with modern science was short-lived, for its author while still young was executed in 1898, in consequence of the abortive *coup d'état* in which he participated.

Another disciple of K'ang Yu-wei who held an eminent place in the intellectual and political world was Liang Ch'i-ch'ao. His influence was more lasting than that of the first two. Like K'ang Yu-wei, he was seeking political reform and wanted to transform the Empire into a constitutional monarchy; but above all he crusaded with his pen to instil in Chinese minds the new ideas from the Occident adapted to his Confucianist convictions. He had thereby a very profound hold on youth, as is witnessed by the memoirs of Hu Shih. Despite his reforming ambitions and his clear patriotism, he never ceased to emphasize the moral point of view. Not a systematic thinker, his ideas aimed at a Confucianist-Buddhist syncretism. In the name of this ideal he preached evolutionism, a liberalism hostile to all despotism, the way of honour, of courage, of the spirit of enterprise, and of the worship of science. Having a well-balanced mind, he denounced both the obstinacy of an unreasonable conservatism and the abuses of an uncurbed radicalism. He groaned to see the onrushing wave of positivist materialism; hence he advocated unceasingly the necessity of religious ideals. In a long essay which has been frequently cited, he expounded all the benefits of a religious belief. He concluded by saying that, if

Japan has produced men of courage, heroes who have brought about the greatness of their country, it is thanks to the philosophy of Wang Yang-ming and to the Buddhist mysticism of the Zen sect. 'Without religion, there is no strength of soul!'

To these three leaders who were a new realization of the classical ideal of the 'philosopher-statesman', it is fitting to add the names of Tseng Kuo-fan, Chang T'ai-yen, and Ku Hung-ming, who were the last representatives of official Confucianism.

Tseng Kuo-fan, more statesman than philosopher, embodied better than the preceding the type of the perfect politician of antiquity: an official of the great class when his services were called upon, and a *literatus* of high culture when he was in retirement. Saviour of the dying dynasty of the Manchus against the T'ai-p'ing rebels (1865), he became conscious of the urgency of reforms in order to safeguard the existence of the nation. He died poor and venerated at Nanking. A middle-of-the-way Confucianist, he was a persevering friend of moderate solutions. His writings, which were models of style, are inspired by noble sentiments. Thus, when he was viceroy of Hopei, he exhorted aspiring officials to heroism, charging them to prepare themselves for service to the State by self-abnegation, abstinence and sacrifice.

Chang T'ai-yen, contrary to the preceding who were trained in the school of Wang Yang-ming, began by adopting the sceptical and disabused attitude of the Taoist Chuang Tzu with regard to civilization. Imbued with liberalism, Chang preached the naturalist politics of *laissez-faire*, the classic theory of Taoism. In consequence he was as much opposed to Confucianian traditionalism as to Occidental ideas. Adopting the theories of transformism, he derived from them an abstract system as a philosophy of life. For him the progress of civilization was the portent of a recrudescence of evil, of sufferings for humanity, and so he had nothing but contempt for the scientific culture of the Occident. Complete renunciation of civilization seemed to him the only means of obtaining universal emancipation. This attitude, so eminently Taoistic, led straight to anarchy. Perhaps Chang T'ai-yen took stock of himself later, for at the end of his life he turned to Confucianism, and even extolled the merits of Wang Yang-ming. On the whole, his work is a harmonization of Taoism with Confucianism: he tried to correct the defects of the one by the excellences of the other. But his influence was never as profound as that of K'ang Yu-wei or Liang Ch'i-ch'ao.

Ku Hung-ming, although more widely known abroad due to his books written in English, is in reality less celebrated in his own country than the preceding: he is not even mentioned in the histories of the modern philosophical movement in China. What has made him read abroad, is his criticism of Occidental civilization—one loves to know the opinion of a Chinese on the Occident! As a matter of fact, even though he tried to harmonize the two civilizations, to complement the one by the other, he remained very much persuaded of the spiritual superiority of Confucianism and was scornful of Occidental materialism.

Such were the leaders of Chinese thought at the end of the nineteenth century, those who were, in different degrees, a real influence on their times. All knew that it was necessary to change something in the governmental machine, but remained faithful to the Empire: all knew that it was necessary to borrow from the Occident its scientific spirit, its spirit of organization, whatever made for strength and material greatness; but all wanted to conserve at all costs the Confucian morality which had in the past brought about the strength and greatness of China. They reckoned that Confucianism had still its word to say in modern times, and were convinced that the welfare of humanity depended upon putting this morality into practice throughout the world. Apart from certain excesses of language in the youthful writings of one or the other, one generally finds from their pens nothing other than eulogy of the moral virtues, mainly after the tradition of Wang Yang-ming, their principal inspiration. It is not without a little melancholy that one re-reads their writings, for they still believed in the primacy of the ideal, of the spirit.

Time, however, marches on. We turn the page. The twentieth century multiplied contacts with the foreigner. Despite the brake which these men attempted to put on Occidentalism, the latter was to end by causing an eruption in the world of ideas and provoking a real intellectual revolution. Let us try, then, to penetrate into the chaos of theories and systems which were clashing together in the course of the first half of the twentieth century, and to appreciate the importance of each in the general evolution of thought. For the convenience of the exposition we shall attempt to make out this balance sheet in three stages. In the first part we shall sketch a general description of the movement of ideas, while emphasizing the principal controversies which have brought to grips the great thinkers of the period. In the two latter parts we shall devote our-selves to the study of the schools of thought and of their leaders, the authors whose thought is of Oriental derivation, along with the philosophers indebted to Occidental thought.

1. Stanislas le Gall, *Le Philosophe Tschou Hi, Sa Doctrine, Son Influence* (*Variétés Sinologiques*), Shanghai, 1894, p. 24.

2. Léon Wieger, *Prodromes* (vol. 1 of *La Chine Moderne*, Hien-hien, 1931), p. 15.

3. *Tr. note:* It seems necessary to clarify this statement by explaining that K'ang Yu-wei had convinced the Kuang Hsü Emperor of the necessity for reforms, and over a period of three months the Emperor issued a series of edicts embodying K'ang's ideas. The real *coup d'état* was that of the Empress Dowager, who acceded to the urgings of the conservative party, and stepped in to remove the Emperor from power.

4. *Tr. note:* The first draft of this work, under the title *Universal Principles of Mankind* 人 類 公 理 , was written in 1884–5. It was expanded by K'ang Yu-wei in later years, and was probably completed in 1902. Parts I and II, constituting about one-third of the whole, were published in *Pu Jen Tsa Chih* 不 忍 雜 誌 , a magazine edited by K'ang, in 1913. The author was from the outset very reluctant to allow publication of this extremely radical work, and it was not published in its entirety until 1935, long after his death.

PART ONE

THE MOVEMENT OF IDEAS
FROM 1898 TO 1950

THE history of Chinese thought in this half-century may itself be divided into two well characterized periods. One, which extends from 1898 to about 1927, is dominated by the positivist, scientific current. The other, which goes from 1927 to the present, is plainly under the sway of Marxist ideas. Beside these two principal currents, there co-existed various idealistic systems whose authors, as we shall see by the following, are often more profound and more original than their materialist colleagues. These, however, are only brilliant individuals who do not represent the main currents of opinion.

Darwinian and Spencerian evolutionism

Already at the end of the nineteenth century, as we have noted, the Confucianist thinkers had taken an interest in the evolutionist doctrines and had attempted to adapt them to their moral system. But the true introduction of evolutionism into China dates from the translation of Thomas Huxley's book, *Evolution and Ethics*, in 1898, by Yen Fu. This translation was immensely famous in China, especially after 1902. Hu Shih, who was then a mere schoolboy, notes in his memoirs that his juvenile enthusiasm was shared by the rest of the country: 'After its appearance Huxley's book made the round of China and became the bedside book of the students.'[1] The book was actually adopted as a manual of Chinese in certain schools, as much for the very well polished style as for the substance. A whole series of expressions taken from Huxley, such as 'the struggle for existence', 'natural selection', and 'the survival of the fittest', became current terms which were applied to external political events as, for example, to the military disasters of China and of

19

Russia. Yen Fu prolonged the fortunes of evolutionism by translating Spencer's *The Study of Sociology*, as well as the classic works of Stuart Mill, Hume, Adam Smith, Montesquieu, and E. Jenks. However, his thought evolved, in a sense, inversely to his times: radical at the start, it became ensuingly conservative and fiercely opposed to the anti-Manchu movement. Yen Fu was moreover only a translator, and never attempted a personal synthesis. Even though he had started the infatuation for transformist doctrines, he was not the principal specialist in those doctrines.

The true promoter of evolutionism in China was Ma Chün-wu, who translated Darwin's *The Origin of Species* and *The Descent of Man*, as well as various works of Spencer and Haeckel. The translator had studied in Japan and Germany. He was several times a member of the government, or president of a university. In his works he assigned himself the role of interpreter and introducer. Since then many other authors have made themselves apostles of evolutionism. One can say that transformism has become an absolute dogma in Chinese cultural circles, and that it has not suffered any serious eclipse up to the present time.

The anarchism of Kropotkin

However, there have been counter-balances to the influence of evolutionism. Li Shih-tseng (Yü-ying), who studied the biology of Montpellier at the beginning of the century, became a fervent adept of anarchism and translated the *Mutual Aid* of Kropotkin, the great thinker of this movement. Kropotkin's system attempted to be a correction or adaptation of Darwinism to the needs of sociology. According to the author the instinct of mutual aid among men takes its origin from the world of insects and animals. Men, like animals, struggle together in order to live, and their survival depends solely on their mutual assistance: hence, evolution is only the development of mutual aid. About 1905 Li Shih-tseng and some comrades founded a review in Paris, in which was published in instalments his translation of Kropotkin. A witness notes that his faith in anarchism verged on fanaticism. He and his friends Wu Chih-hui and Wang Ching-wei enthusiastically praised their common ideal of liberty and mutual aid for the welfare of humanity. A little later this group of friends, who were in the beginning at the

University of Outremer, entered into relations with Sun Yat-sen on behalf of the Chinese students at Lyons and affiliated themselves with his party, the future Kuomintang.

Another politically important figure, Chou Fo-hai, flirted momentarily with anarchism, and also translated *Mutual Aid* into Chinese. This passion did not last with him, and he afterwards entered the embryonic Communist party of 1921. Later he joined the Kuomintang and finally ended up as mayor of Shanghai under the Wang Ching-wei government which collaborated with Japan. The man was not without merit, but he was a restless soul, incapable of settling himself down.

Fundamentally then, anarchism was only a youthful transgression with these men, since, when they arrived at the age of maturity, they rejected it. It lasted longer in the case of a writer who is very popular today, the celebrated novelist Pa Chin. One day as a child he chanced to acquire a work of Kropotkin, perhaps *Mutual Aid*, and the reading of this book provoked in him such enthusiasm that he undertook the translation of the complete works of this thinker. That occurred in 1920. Since then Pa Chin has translated *My Autobiography*, *Bread and Liberty*, and *The Source and Development of Ethics*, and his admiration has not slackened. Pa Chin, like the others, is attracted to anarchism by the dreamy humanitarianism of Kropotkin, believing one finds in his theories the secret of universal happiness for humanity.

The voluntarism of Nietzsche

At the time when Li Shih-tseng was enamoured of Kropotkin's thought, another scholar, Wang Kuo-wei, had published his *Essays of Ching-an* (靜 菴 文 集 (1905)), in which he introduced the German voluntarism of Schopenhauer and Nietzsche. More under the influence of Schopenhauer than of Nietzsche, he seems to have been a victim of his master's pessimism. On May 3rd, 1927, as the victories of the 'Southerners' seemed to forecast the collapse of the government of Peking, Wang Kuo-wei, seized by despair, threw himself into a lake of the Imperial Palace. He was only fifty years of age. Different from his rivals, he was a true thinker, not merely a translator.

Another author who was greatly influenced by Nietzschean

thought is Li Shih-ts'en. After studying in Japan, he returned to his own country, where he became a university professor and editor of important reviews. In 1928 he undertook a trip to Europe and stayed in France and Germany. There he came in contact with various influential university people, and ardently studied current philosophical problems. In his writings, despite their unsystematic character, he showed himself superior to his predecessors as a thinker. He concentrated especially on the philosophy of life, and on the comparative study of Oriental and Occidental philosophies. In homage to the masters of his thought, Bergson and Nietzsche, he dedicated two numbers of his review, *Min To* (民 鐸). To explain Nietzsche he also wrote a work entitled *Brief Outline of the Philosophy of the Superman* (超 人 哲 學 學 說), as well as many magazine articles. His critical presentation extends also to most of the other important thinkers and systems of the period, as much the Occidental as the Chinese. But the trip to Europe seems to have brought about a new orientation of his thought. Indeed, after his return to China in 1930, he stupefied his friends, when he wrote in an important review that 'the philosophy of the future will be scientific materialism', otherwise called dialectical materialism. In truth his latest works, a *Treatise on Philosophy* (哲 學 大 綱),[1] and *Ten Lectures on Chinese Philosophy* (中 國 哲 學 十 講)[1] (both published in 1933), are dominated by the principles of his new belief: he judges everything as a function of the Marxist dialectic. This *volte-face* is in the spirit of the times. He is a man of transition: this radical evolution of his thought is a reflection of the upheavals going on in all Chinese minds around the crucial years 1928 and 1929. Many others imitated him.

The first interpreter of Marxism: Ch'en Tu-hsiu

Thus the thought of Nietzsche had its hour in vogue, like the anarchism of Kropotkin. If we have caused an anachronism by mixing in Pa Chin and Li Shih-ts'en with the authors of the beginning of the twentieth century, it is only for the convenience of our exposition. Let us now go back. The philosophical fever which marked the first years of the twentieth century, was followed by an almost complete calm from 1905 to 1915. Even the backwash of the political revolution of 1911, which replaced the Empire by the

Republic, did not have any immediate repercussion in the philosophical world. Despite all the changes, spiritual evolution pursued its own way. Two slogans then occupied the field of thought: Science, and Democracy. The fermentation of ideas provoked by these two terms which seemed the panacea for modern times, ended by bringing about an extremely violent campaign against Confucianism. For the partisans of the Republic the fate of Confucianism was tied in with the Empire. Its moral and political philosophy was the firmest ideological support of the old regime, and because of this fact it shared in the general reprobation involving the fallen dynasty. Furthermore, 'Confucianism' was synonymous with conservative, backward, stereotyped thought; it was an enemy of progress and anti-scientific. Therefore it was necessary in the name of science and democracy to destroy this emblem of obscurantism and despotism. Such were the reasons alleged by the champions of the anti-Confucian campaign. The leader of this controversy, which agitated intellectual circles especially between 1915 and 1920, was Ch'en Tu-hsiu, editor of *La Jeunesse Nouvelle* (新青年), the most influential review of the period.[2] He acquired by his articles a preponderant place among the thinkers of the time. It is he also who was the firmest supporter of Hu Shih in his campaign for a 'literary reform'. Imbued with democratic theories which he had derived from France, Ch'en Tu-hsiu did not cease to repeat: 'Republican government in politics and science in the domain of ideas, these seem to me the two treasures of modern civilization.'[3] Now, according to him, Confucianism and Republican government are incompatible. Why? Because Confucianism exercised a monopoly fatal to the development of the country. It is no longer adapted to modern exigencies: the tyranny of its moral notions over men's minds is contrary to the democratic ideal, which seeks to liberate man from all bondage, spiritual or material. This line of argument evidently shocked many readers of his review. And so he found himself constrained to distinguish thus: he did not mean to abolish all morals, but only the Confucian morals. He contends that ethics like all the sciences is relative, evolving with the times, and hence he wishes to destroy only the Confucian concept of absolute ethics. He concludes: 'The old ethics is no longer adapted to the modern world, which is ruled by economy.'[4] Thus, he ended up by asserting the primacy of the economic—that essential law of Marxism.

Thus his is also an ideological evolution. After having battled fervently for the triumph of republican ideas, he suddenly perceives the inanity of this ideal. In 1920 he writes: 'The republic cannot give happiness to the masses.'[5] And again: 'Evolution goes from feudalism to republicanism and from republicanism to communism. I have said that the republic has failed and that feudalism has been reborn, but I hope that soon the feudal forces will be wiped out again by democracy and the latter by socialism . . . for I am convinced that the creation of a proletarian state is the most urgent revolution in China.'[6] Completely imbued with this creed, he henceforth consecrated his powers to the realization of his ideal. It was he who founded the Communist party in 1921, and directed it until 1927. He was called the Chinese Lenin. But the vicissitudes of politics were cruel to him. He encountered a mounting opposition, his adversaries stripped him of the presidency and even expelled him from the party. However, his faith in Communism remained complete, and he tried to create an opposition movement—later dubbed 'Trotskyist'—which did nothing but vegetate. To complete his misfortunes, the Nanking government threw him into prison. Liberated by the Sino-Japanese war in 1937, he died unnoticed in 1942. *Sic transit gloria mundi!* His writings on behalf of Marxism had only been isolated essays without systematic character.

Hu Shih and the pragmatism of Dewey

Before becoming a mere organ of the nascent Communist party, the review *La Jeunesse* under the aegis of Ch'en Tu-hsiu had thrust itself on the attention of the public by its campaign in favour of the *pai hua* or spoken language, to supplant the *ku-wen* or classical style, so concise and so obscure. Indeed, it was in the columns of *La Jeunesse* that a young student, Hu Shih, published his manifestoes in favour of a Literary Revolution (1917). Upon his return from studying in America, he won fame at the very outset. By this campaign he acquired and retained in history the name of 'Father of the Literary Revolution'. However, it is not by this title that we wish to speak of him here. Hu Shih is also the introducer of pragmatism into China, and more especially that of Dewey, his former teacher. Convinced that the methods of intellectual work should be scientific, he believed that in philosophy the pragmatic method alone merited this name. In his view it is nothing less than the art of the scholar in his laboratory: 'To examine the facts attentively, to risk a hypothesis boldly, finally to strive to find the proofs.'[7] However, this discipline cannot be used unilaterally, for it proves inefficacious in judging theories or beliefs. It is therefore necessary to complete it by the historical method. Every belief occupies time and space, and to judge of its value it is necessary to look at the consequences. The only criterion of truth, then, will be the practically begotten result; whence the error of all metaphysical speculation. 'Now, we are conscious that the point of departure of philosophy should be the study of life, thought being only an instrument.'[8] This is why the name *instrumentalism* is sometimes given to Dewey's thought. As life is in perpetual evolution, as the environment changes ceaselessly, so truth must also evolve—it cannot be other than relative, transitory, spatial. Thus is Darwinian evolutionism adapted to the study of speculative and moral problems.

Armed with this pragmatic method, Hu Shih devoted himself to a critical work on the ancient philosophy. In his *History of Chinese Philosophy* (中 國 哲 學 史), of which only the first volume has appeared (1919), he passes in review the two most influential schools of antiquity, Confucianism and Taoism. Since he is in love with liberty and individualism, he finds that Confucianism was wrong in teaching subordination to sovereign, father, state and family. Since he believes in the necessity of striving to dominate nature, he blames Taoism for teaching us only to enjoy it and advocating 'laissez-faire'. 'On reading his book,' remarks Fung Yu-lan, 'one cannot help but see that for him Chinese civilization has been entirely led astray.'[9] The philosophy of Mo Ti, however, found favour in Hu's eyes, not by reason of its high moral value, but because he thought he found there some elements of pragmatism.

The authority of Hu Shih, great though it was, was not in itself sufficient to give the popularity to this system which it attained in 1920 and afterwards. What contributed still more effectively, was the sojourn in China of Dewey himself from 1919 to 1921. In the course of these two years the American philosopher spoke in the universities of eleven provinces, explaining his ideas, especially on the subject of education. The texts of his lectures were published in the reviews of the period with critical evaluations. This greatly extended the effect of his speaking. So, when the lecturer re-embarked for America, Hu Shih wrote dithyrambically: 'We can say that, since the meeting of China and the Occident, there has not been a single foreigner who has had such an influence on the world of Chinese thought.'[10] This judgment was correct at the time, for infatuation with pragmatism was very ardent in those years. Today it is no longer the same: Dewey is eclipsed, although his influence in China still abides. Because of the large number of Chinese students in America, there have been many who have been impregnated with his doctrines and have returned enthusiastic for the American teacher.

The neo-realism of Russell

Shortly after Dewey's visit, the English philosopher, Bertrand Russell, also came to China. This event also aroused much interest. At least four or five of his works were translated into Chinese. However, although he has been many times presented and commented upon in the reviews, he never attained the vogue of his American colleague. His interpreter to the public was Chang Shen-fu, who published many articles about him and taught his theories at the University of Peking. Chang, however, was not only a specialist on Russell. His philosophical method is an amalgam of dialectical materialism and Russellian objectivism.

Thus, one sees that there was an intense philosophical boiling and bubbling around about 1920. The introduction of Occidental systems of philosophy provoked a feverish curiosity. But if the Occidentalists dominated the field of thought, the Orientalists did not consider themselves beaten. The arguments between the two camps were incessant in these years. In the quarrel over Confucianism one saw the greatest intellectual authorities enter the lists to protect the milleniums-old heritage of Chinese thought. There was, for example, K'ang Yu-wei. Not long ago ahead of his times, and even very daring in certain of his conceptions, he found himself today quite outdone.

The defender of Confucianism: Liang Shu-ming

Another defender of tradition, Liang Shu-ming, arose to protest against the iconoclasts, against the scorners of the national thought *à la* Ch'en Tu-hsiu or Hu Shih. A little after the appearance of the *History of Chinese Philosophy* of the latter (1919), Liang Shu-ming published his famous book, *The Civilizations of Orient and Occident and Their Philosophies* (東 西 文 化 及 其 哲 學) (1922).

Before that, in 1917 and 1918, the out-and-out champions of Occidentalism, Ch'en Tu-hsiu and his friend, Li Ta-chao, had each on his own part instituted comparisons between Orient and Occident. For Ch'en Tu-hsiu, the principal difference between the two civilizations lay not so much in greater or less material prosperity as in the quality of thought being better or less adapted to modern times. For Li Ta-chao, on the contrary, the characteristic point was the question of action and repose: the Occident had put the accent on action and the Orient on repose. Hence Chinese civilization was no longer well-adapted; it must return to the cultivation of the 'scientific and democratic' spirit, which had brought about the strength of the modern Occident.

In 1919, Liang Ch'i-ch'ao returned from Europe, where he had travelled about in order to review the new conditions issuing from the world war. He returned horrified with what he had seen, and recorded his impressions in his book, *Recollections of a Trip to Europe* (歐 遊 心 影 錄), in which he proclaims the bankruptcy of science. In substance he says that the Europeans have believed in its omnipotence and announced the coming of a golden age. Now science has culminated in only material development: on the spiritual plain there has been total failure. The material progress indeed has created an inhuman, mechanized life, and has brought about the throes of this gigantic war in which the world remains twitching. We must conclude, therefore, as to the excellence of Oriental civilization, that it is materially backward, but spiritually superior.

Plainly in accord with this opinion Liang Shu-ming undertakes in his book thoroughly to discuss the problem of Oriental and Occidental philosophies. According to him civilization is divided into three stages, corresponding to three attitudes of life. In the first stage man tries to gain the objects indispensable to his needs, whence an attitude of striving, of progress, of getting ahead, which is that of the Occident. In the second stage man establishes that the excess of desires is finally injurious to his happiness, so he seeks an equilibrium, a harmonization of the passions, which is the appanage of Chinese civilization. Finally, in the highest stage, he comes to see the inanity of lusts, the impossibility of finding happiness in even a moderated attempt to satisfy them. Hence he goes back and thinks to find happiness by divesting himself of them: that is the Hindu wisdom. In a word, the Occident seeks the satisfaction of its desires, China their limitation, India their suppression. Between these three attitudes it is necessary to make a choice. Since Chinese civilization adopts the happy medium, it is preferable, the other two being manifestly exaggerated. 'In short, it is necessary to reject Hindu civilization as useless, radically to change the Occidental, and to return to our tradition after having criticized it.'[11] Liang prophesies: 'The world-civilization of the future will be the renovated Chinese civilization.'[12]

Such are the great principles. In practice, in detail, how must the Occident be rejected and China regained? The concepts of 'science' and 'democracy', characteristic of the modern Occident, are to be conserved, but corrected. In order to take up 'science' completely afresh, and to prevent it from committing new crimes, it is necessary to imbue it with the Confucian spirit of Wang Yang-ming, which is essentially benevolent, a source of unselfish actions, without distinction of mine and thine. By this means science can purge itself of its disastrous utilitarianism.

As to the right mode of government, Liang proposes an economy based on rural reconstruction. To this effect he advocates the return to the village of the elite who have deserted it, to work in common accord with the toilers for the solution of local problems. When agricultural prosperity can be assured, then we can think of industrial prosperity. This is why Liang founded at Chouping, Shantung, a social experimental centre with an Institute of Rural Reconstruction, and later established a second one in Honan. In those high schools he devoted himself above all to the moral training of his students. Thus did he abandon discussion for action. He was considered the leader of the Rural Reconstruction party.

Now, disgusted with politics, he has retired from action and has plunged again into study and personal meditation. Asked to give his advice on his country's civil war, he wrote on January 12, 1947, in a Tientsin paper: 'The fundamental task of politics lies in the cultural problem . . . If a solution is not found for that, it will be impossible to bring about accord on political questions.'[13]

Upon the appearance of this book, the ideas expressed therein provoked much discussion. The leaders of Occidentalism criticized this article sharply, and there was much ink spilled over the Orient-Occident problem.

The controversy 'science v. philosophy of life'

The tumult in the intellectual world had not yet died down when there arose a new controversy which was also to become very sharp. This was called 'The Quarrel between Metaphysicians and Scientists.' The occasion of the fray was a lecture given at Tsinghua University in Peking on February 14, 1923, by a young professor who was a disciple of Liang Ch'i-ch'ao. This was Chang Chün-mai, who was to become famous in the political world under the name of Carson Chang. This young professor, who had studied in Japan and Germany, declared in his lecture that day that the philosophy of life could in no manner be governed by scientific, deterministic principles, but that it had its origin in the intuitive moral conscience of man, under the impulsion of the free will. 'Science cannot solve the problems of life. The great philosophers of history are those who have tried to find a solution to the problems of life. Among us there has been a series of philosophers, from Confucius and Mencius to the Sung and Ming neo-Confucian literati, who have produced the great spiritual civilization of China.'[14] This, after all, was resuming from another angle the discussion on civilizations started by Liang Shu-ming, and Chang clearly was advocating the moral philosophy of Confucianism, preaching the necessity of a moral ideal against the partisans of scientific positivism.

His opponents were not slow in taking up the gauntlet. On the following April 12, Ting Wen-chiang, professor of geology at the University of Peking, attacked Chang Chün-mai in an article entitled 'Science and Metaphysics', accusing him of combining the Bergsonian intuitionism of *l'élan vital* with the intuitionism of Wang

Yang-ming, in order to resuscitate an out-dated and disastrous idealistic metaphysics. 'The object of science is to eliminate personal subjective prejudices and to search for the truth which is general and universal. . . . Science is all-sufficient, not so much in its subject matter as in the manner of procedure.'[15] Chang Chün-mai retorted: 'It is time that thinkers go beyond the confines of empiricism and rationalism. Manifestly there is knowledge outside of science. The field of knowledge is not limited to science. There are some truths and some hypotheses in philosophy, in aesthetics and in religion which cannot be verified by scientific criteria. . . . Science is far from being omnipotent: it is limited in its scope as in its methods.'[16] By this defiance towards science—which he accused of materializing the world—Chang added to the criticisms of Liang Ch'i-ch'ao and Liang Shu-ming against Occidental civilization, and taught the superiority of the Chinese conception. It is not astonishing, therefore, that Liang Ch'i-ch'ao should descend into the arena to come to the succour of his disciple: 'The driving force of life is feeling . . . so how can we judge the heroes of love? . . . If human life be under the jurisdiction of science in logical matters, it does not depend on logic at all in matters which concern feeling.'[17] Another friend of Chang Chün-mai, the philosopher Chang Tung-sun, also took part in the dispute, and with perhaps more success. In his capacity of metaphysician, he naturally took up the defence of metaphysics: 'The role of philosophy is hereafter to criticize the sciences. . . . It has an independent place, an end and a method proper to it . . . whereas science should describe, not interpret the universe. It answers the "how", not the "why".'[18]

Despite these illustrious names marshalled on his side, Chang Chün-mai was against the majority opinion: a fact quite symptomatic of the spirit of the times and the growing vogue of positivism. As a result he threw himself into politics and founded a party which was at first called 'National-Socialist', and then 'Social-Democrat'. This was the descendant of various political groups created by his teacher, Liang Ch'i-ch'ao, opposing the T'ung-meng-hui, or future Kuomintang of Sun Yat-sen. But this new party chief never recruited a great number of members, for he was more an intellectual than a man of action. His political influence, however, was not negligible. Some years afterwards he opened and directed the first

Political Institute at Woosung, his native place, near Shanghai. In this way he made many political contacts. Still later, during the Sino-Japanese war, while he was a refugee in Szechuan, he founded an Institute of National Culture, which was also a centre of Confucianism. In short he remained faithful all his life to his first ideas. Strongly influenced by Bergson and Eucken, he also kept in line with the national tradition, for with him, Bergsonian idealism and Confucian idealism only complemented each other. From the political point of view, despite the similarity of name between his party and the National-Socialist party of Hitler, he did not intend to copy Naziism. Chang Chün-mai was a partisan of state socialism: for him, the nation comes first, and socialism itself is subordinate to it. But his idealistic socialism is aligned more closely with the Communist party than with the Kuomintang.

The aestheticism of Ts'ai Yüan-p'ei

Another important figure of the period is that of Ts'ai Yüan-p'ei, who was for a long time chancellor of the University of Peking, and on several occasions Minister of Education. Like K'ang Yu-wei and Liang Ch'i-ch'ao, he was at one and the same time an ardent innovator and a convinced Confucianist, even though he opposed the attempt of the conservatives who wished to proclaim Confucianism the State Religion. At Leipzig he had studied aesthetics, experimental psychology, and the history of civilizations. Interested in the moral problem, he wrote a *History of Chinese Ethics*, and translated Paulsen's *System of Ethics*, but he distinguished himself above all by his theory of art as the substitute for religion. According to the conclusion he drew from his studies of comparative civilization, all religion arises from the imagination, which seeks consolation from the miseries of life. Now, he thinks, if the adepts of these religions believe in dogmas which are often incoherent, it is by reason of their picturesque symbolism. Hence this formula: 'It is art which causes the attraction of religions.'[19] Indeed, he remarks, religion has always used beautiful sites for the establishment of its temples, which have often been masterpieces of art. Now that the era of religions is ended, could we not with advantage substitute a purely aesthetic teaching for the religious teaching of the past? A beautiful concert, a beautiful tragedy, do they not elevate the soul as much as a religious service? And in nature, what themes of profound emotion! The immense ocean, the starry heavens, the great landscapes of mountains, are they not elevating of themselves? Moreover, if one considers the general evolution of civilization it seems apparent, viewing the decline of the religious spirit, that art and literature are abandoning religion completely, after the example of science. 'It is almost certain', he believes, 'that man will end by deriving the consolations of life from the enjoyment of beauty, aesthetics having replaced religion.'[20]

This religion of *aestheticism*, stated in modern terms by Ts'ai Yüan-p'ei, was not a novelty in China. Had it not been the practical belief of thousands of aesthetes in the course of the centuries? The artists of antiquity took pleasure in showing this attitude, as is seen by these words of a poet: 'I go alone, I intoxicate myself with contemplation of the blue sky, the brilliant moon and the numberless stars, I lose all notion of time and space.'[21] In short, if Ts'ai Yüan-p'ei has given to aestheticism a special form, fundamentally he has only sanctioned an old tradition—a tradition which is, moreover, far from being lost, as we shall see farther on.

First applications of the materialistic dialectic

All of these theories and controversies date from around 1920, either a little before, or a little after. The moment has now arrived to take up the introduction of Marxism into China.

We have already said a few words about Ch'en Tu-hsiu and his associate Li Ta-chao, the first exponents of the great Marxist theses in China. As early as 1919, they published their essays in the columns of *La Jeunesse*. In that year they devoted an entire number of the review to studying the cardinal points of dialectical materialism; and thereafter almost every issue carried a few dissertations on the subject. After 1921, *La Jeunesse* became a mere organ of Marxist propaganda under the direction of Li Ta-chao, who replaced his friend as editor. But the new editor was to have a tragic fate. In 1927 he was seized and shot by the military authorities of the Peking government for social agitation. Among his early collaborators two names should be mentioned in view of their notoriety in the ranks of Marxism—those of Li Ta and Li Chi.

Although the propagation of the new ideas was intensified during the following years, they did not as yet draw much attention. The first to employ Marxist methodology as a tool in their work were mostly writers. Kuo Mo-jo, the leader of a romantic literary school, was the first of the writers to formulate the principles of the dialectical materialism to which he has been devoted since 1925. In the light of his faith he scrutinizes the antiquity of China, and draws from it entirely new conclusions: 'When one wishes to speak of antiquity,' he says, 'it does not suffice to study the written documents and the old historians. It is necessary first of all to know Marx and Engels, for they give us the key to all interpretation to come, that is to say, the materialistic point of view. It is necessary then to get rid of the ordinary, classical, self-styled scientific method of the historians, which is in fact influenced by their prejudices.'[22] Although first and foremost a poet and dramatist, Kuo Mo-jo has worked in almost all fields, and usually with ability: archaeology, economics, philosophy, sociology. So far as philosophy is concerned, he has collected his critical studies in two books, *The Bronze Age* (青 銅 時 代) and *Ten Critiques* (十 批 判 書), both appearing in 1945. It goes without saying that his conclusions do not at all match with those of other specialists on antiquity.

Kuo Mo-jo was also one of the leaders of the controversy on Chinese society which began in 1928. Starting from the primacy of economics, the basic principle of Marxist ideology, several controversialists tried to determine the different periods of Chinese history according to the mode of production. They were unanimous in declaring that primitive society constituted a communist society, and the present a capitalist society; but they were not in accord in fixing and characterizing the various intermediary periods. In reality the stakes of the battle were of little consequence; but the discussion revealed to what an extent Marxism was in the forefront of Chinese thought. Kuo Mo-jo combined the fruit of his meditations in a *Study of Ancient Chinese Society* (中 國 古 代 社 會 研 究) (1932). Assuredly his multiple genius which permitted him to take up so many different fields is a unique case in China. Hence he has very naturally been nominated to the post which the new Chinese Communist government has entrusted to him, that of President of the Cultural Federation for all China—a body including nearly fifty philosophers, historians, writers, sociologists, etc. As an even more flattering distinction, he has at the same time been named one of the four vice-presidents of the Central Political Committee.

The long controversy between Marxists and anti-Marxists

More important was the ideological battle which started in 1929 and was very prolonged. In this, it was a question of the triumphing of principles involving two different conceptions of the world. The articles for or against Marxism, published by the various authors who took part in the controversy, were combined in two volumes through the care of two philosophers who may be considered as the leaders of the combatants. Chang Tung-sun published *The Controversy over Dialectical Materialism* (唯 物 辯 證 法 論 戰) (1934), in which he brought together especially the anti-Marxist studies. The following year Yeh Ch'ing replied with his *Philosophical Controversies* (哲 學 論 戰) (1935), in which, taking the opposing side, he inserted principally the pro-Marxist essays.

The quarrel between Marxists and scientists

That controversy had scarcely ended from the general lassitude of the authors than another arose, still more furious—this time, within the materialist camp. Yeh Ch'ing, who had fought so hard for the cause, was suddenly and violently taken to task by his colleagues, who accused him of betraying Marx. Indeed, even though he had a great esteem for Marxist thought, he was not entirely subservient to Marx, did not consider him as a unique prophet, and did not hurl him exclusively against other thinkers. Such was the origin of the drama. Yeh Ch'ing defended his cause with vigour and with an incredible fecundity. In our opinion, moreover, he was much superior to his attackers in dialectical power. He compiled his essays in two volumes: *The Controversies of the New Philosophy* (新 哲 學 論 戰 集) (1936) and *Struggles in the Developing of the New Philosophy* (為 發 展 新 哲 學 而 戰) (1937). During the two years that the controversy lasted there were as yet no signs of it slackening when the Sino-Japanese war broke out. This event brought an end to the pen-jousting, and the adversaries were separated. The Marxist thinkers were divided into two principal groups: those of the one took refuge in Yenan, the capital of Soviet China in the north of Shensi, the other followed the government in its removals, at first to Hankow, then to Chungking.

At Yenan, in 1938, the Marxist philosophers, who were reunited under the direction of Ai Ssu–ch'i (艾 思 奇), the great adversary of Yeh Ch'ing in the preceding controversy, founded the 'Society of the New Philosophy'. This society published its studies in the review *Chinese Culture* (中 國 文 化). It was in this review that the leader of the Communist party, Mao Tse-tung, published a famous article, entitled 'The government and culture of the new democracy' (1940). This document became the political and philosophical charter which the Marxist intellectuals took as the basis of their studies, and on which they wrote fervent commentaries. At Chungking, in 1939, a parallel association was created around the review *Theory and Reality* (理 論 與 現 實). The writers were all well-known Marxists—philosophers, sociologists, historians, economists. This was at the time certainly the best written Marxist doctrinal review which had appeared in China. After the victory over Japan in 1945, it still continued to be published for a while; however, it suddenly disappeared one fine day, doubtless by order of the Nationalist government. At Shanghai philosophical activity abated. In 1940 two small periodicals were published in succession. One was extinguished after the second number, the other, which started in October 1940, under the name *Philosophy* (哲 學), lasted more than a year. Modest in format, it was nevertheless very vital and original, whence its good fortune. But all Marxist activity ceased on the day the Japanese invaded the Concessions, with the declaration of the Pacific war, on December 8, 1941.

After the victory, when the Nationalist government re-entered Shanghai, free literary expression recommenced. Then the intellectual forces of Marxism appeared greater than ever. In spite of covert censorship, the windows of the book shops were nearly all largely occupied by works of Marxist inspiration. Even the government book stores offered to the visitor examples of notoriously Marxist books; 'One must do business,' the bookseller would say to those who expressed astonishment about it to him. As one can see, it would be vain to question the seductiveness of Marxism within intellectual circles. One notes a quantitative and qualitative increase in this direction between 1935 and 1945.

The philosophy of the Kuomintang

The Nationalist government of Nanking, at the same time that it was keeping a close surveillance over, and even harshly repressing, the partisans of dialectical materialism, itself tried various methods to combat its adversaries in the realm of ideas. For this purpose Chiang Kai-shek inaugurated his 'New Life' movement, on February 19, 1934, at Nanchang—a movement which was more than mere anti-Communist propaganda, for he intended to give the nation a new spirit. Pointing out as examples the order and discipline of the Germans and the Japanese, he desired to infuse a new soul, the utmost in energy, will, order and integrity, while at the same time re-engendering trust in the ancestral virtues. 'The weakness of China', he said in the inaugural address, 'is due to the fact that we have completely forgotten our ancient virtues. . . . In order to change our bad social habits, we must go forward in a great co-operative effort.' To that end he summarized the doctrine of the movement by proposing the four Confucian virtues of sincerity, reason, honesty, and honour. Huge meetings were held in order to launch the 'New Life', and then a detailed programme came out, giving concrete means for prompting the cultivation of order and discipline. The great cities of China each in turn held propaganda congresses, and the movement was progressing peacefully when the Sino-Japanese war crushed all its efforts in 1937.

While the Generalissimo was striving to restore a soul to the popular masses, a collective national *ésprit*, another eminent member of the Kuomintang, at one time the head of the legal wing, Ch'en Li-fu, published the text of lectures delivered before the students of the Central Political Institute under the title *Vitalism* (唯生論) (1934). This was a metaphysical essay which attempted to place the Three People's Principles of Sun Yat-sen on systematic bases. His speculation proceeded from the central concept 'life', and claimed thus to resolve the eternal opposition between materialism and idealism. It was inspired largely by the Bergsonian theory of *l'élan vital* and by the works of Hans Driesch and Eucken, that is to say, by the authors who were in reaction against the materialist conception of science. In fact Ch'en Li-fu was trying to bring certain classical virtues of Confucianism back into favour. But his system was not lacking in weak points, and his adversaries made great sport of attacking it. Ultimately his attempt did not evoke any great response: aside from a few magazines which were mouthpieces of the Kuomintang, and two or three authors who tried to exploit these new ideas, it had only a small influence. The movement lasted only a few years, its demise being hastened by the breaking out of the war between China and Japan. Its initiator, although not a philosopher by profession, did not limit himself to this essay. In July 1944, he resumed and completed his system with a work entitled *The Origin of Life* (生 之 原 理). One of his commentators, in a small tract which he devoted to the 'vitalist' epistemology, remarked explicitly that the aim of his metaphysics was to furnish a philosophy and a spiritual arm to the Kuomintang in its battle against Communism.

The Chinese Philosophical Society

As for the mass of the professional philosophers—generally university professors, who did not let themselves become carried away by more or less explicitly political considerations, and who wrote technical works of philosophical research—they foregathered around the review *Philosophical Critique* (哲 學 評 論), which was in existence for ten years from 1927 to 1937. This review brought together all the important names of modern philosophy, such as Fung Yu-lan, Chang Tung-sun, Chang Chün-mai, Hu Shih, etc., on its editorial committee. Some years later, in 1935, the Chinese Philosophical Society was founded, which today numbers 120 members, and whose president was the most famous contemporary philosopher of China, Fung Yu-lan. This society held annual meetings in the beginning, and the reports of these congresses, discussions between members, and communications of authors were published in the *Philosophical Critique*. The studies published in this review most often concerned the thinkers and systems of the modern Occident or the sages of Chinese antiquity from the historical or exegetical point of view. In the years which preceded the Sino-Japanese war, the review and the Association kept painstakingly aloof from the Marxist thinkers, for we never come across the

names of celebrated dialectical materialists. Undoubtedly the one
and the other were under the more or less official patronage of the
Kuomintang government. In 1941 there was a new development of
the Philosophical Society, thanks to the establishment of a committee, under the presidency of Ho Lin, for translation of the
important works of Occidental philosophy. Until then translations
were made at random; henceforth, they were done according to a
systematic plan. Thus in recent years were published the *Parmenides
of Plato* by Ch'en K'ang, *The Philosophy of Loyalty of Royce* by Hsieh
Yu-wei, *The Treatise on the Improvement of the Understanding*[23] *of
Spinoza* by Ho Lin, *The Principles of Psychology of William James*
by T'ang Yüeh, *The Classical Moralists of Benjamin Rand, The Spirit
of Modern Philosophy by Royce*, and the *Destiny of Man of Fichte*. . . .

The professors obviously did not teach philosophy to a very large
number of students. In order to consent to specialize in philosophical
studies for four years, a student would necessarily not be ambitious
to find a livelihood: he could only be drawn to it by love of pure
thought. In the whole of China one could find some ten universities
which had special departments of philosophy. Of these ten universities more than half were Protestant. In fact, the forming of Chinese
thinkers at present is almost always completed abroad, in Germany,
England, France, and above all America.

Among the university professors two men are outstanding,
Fung Yu-lan and Chang Tung-sun. Fung Yu-lan is the present
president (1949) of the round 120 members who constitute the
Chinese Philosophical Society, and is certainly the most eminent
representative of modern Chinese thought. He studied philosophy
first at the University of Peking and then in America at Columbia
University. He fell under the influence of pragmatism and of
American neo-realism, even of Marxism; but he is first of all a
disciple of Chu Hsi, the somewhat positivistic commentator on
Confucius. He became famous by the publication of his *History of
Chinese Philosophy* (中 國 哲 學 史) (vol. I, 1931, vol. II,
1934), of which the first volume was translated into English in
1937.[24] Fung's history is considered the most complete work thus
far published, and it has overshadowed the similar work by Hu Shih.
At the same time the critics reproach him, and not unreasonably,
with exaggerating his interpretation of classical Chinese philosophy

in the materialistic sense. His own philosophical system was not evolved and delivered to the public until 1940, in the midst of war. Among the five or six works which showed the various aspects of his thought, the most important is *New Li Hsüeh* (新 理 學) or 'new explanation of Reason (or the Norm)', i.e. the principle of neo-Confucianism in the light of modern philosophy. This has been the most important philosophical event of these past ten years in China.

His rival in celebrity, Chang Tung-sun, leaves ancient Chinese philosophy completely aside and constructs a system based entirely on Occidental thought. He starts out from the Kantian problem of knowledge, to build up little by little what he calls the 'pluralism of knowledge': a synthesis, finally, of Kant and the Americans Lewis and Morgan. As for ethics, he is influenced above all by Wundt. His philosophy is also concerned with politics. We have seen that earlier he was the leader of the intellectual opposition to the rising tide of Marxism. But fifteen years later, his thought underwent a surprising evolution. In 1946 he published three books, the fruit of his incarceration under the Japanese: *Knowledge and Culture* (知 識 與 文 化), *Thought and Society* (思 想 與 社 會), and *Reason and Democracy* (理 性 與 民 主). In these he applies himself to showing that democracy is not only a political regime, but also implies a whole civilization, a progressive attitude of life. Without yet being Marxism, his socialism comes considerably near to it. Still more recently, in 1948, in a little volume entitled *Democracy and Socialism* (民 主 主 義 與 社 會 主 義), he integrates many of the Marxist elements, and shows an esteem for Marx which not long ago he was far from having. Although a former disciple of Liang Ch'i-ch'ao and friend of Chang Chün-mai, with whom he collaborated for so long, he has broken with the small political party which represented the idealistic socialism of his friend. In acknowledgement, the Communist regime has named him a member of the Cultural Federation presided over by Kuo Mo-jo.

Neo-Buddhist philosophy

However, outside of all of these groups and all of these diverse tendencies, there is also a school of thought of which we have not spoken, that of neo-Buddhism. The reason is very simple. Buddhism forms a closed world, apart, without ties with the other systems. If Buddhism as a religion is retrograding with a rather rapid rhythm, it must yet be said that the Buddhist intellectuals have made a considerable effort to modernize and spread Buddhist speculation by drawing inspiration from such Occidental theories as are capable of vivifying it.

The initiator of the movement was a certain Ou-Yang Ching-wu. He was only a layman, and at first a disciple of Wang Yang-ming and neo-Confucianism, for which he always maintained a singular esteem. After having embraced Buddhism, he founded at Nanking 'The Chinese Academy for the Study of Buddhism', destined to restore to favour and to deepen the principles of the Fa-hsiang School, and to re-edit the masterpieces of the *wei shih* (唯 識) philosophy, a complex and subtle system of metaphysics imported from India in ancient times by the famous pilgrim monk Hsüan Tsang. This philosophy has always been regarded as the summit of Buddhist rationalism, and it is the only one which attracts modern speculative and critical minds. Resolutely rationalistic and atheistic, it is inimical to worship. So the partisans of this school declare with Ou-Yang Ching-wu: 'Buddhism is neither a religion nor a philosophy. . . . The Buddhist Law is only the Buddhist Law.'[25]

Ou-Yang Ching-wu was only the forerunner. The greatest theoretician of the school was the bonze T'ai Hsü, who remains the dominant figure of neo-Buddhism. Entering very young into the monastic life, he felt keenly the decadence of his religion and the contempt which surrounded the bonzes, a scorn which he himself shared in part. Intimate with the revolutionary partisans of Sun Yat-sen, he was convinced that it was necessary also to effect a revolution within Buddhism by modernizing it and by breaking with tradition on many points. The bonzes had no idea of social service, did not seek in any way to adapt their doctrine to the exigencies of the times, knew nothing of the sciences or Occidental philosophy, and lived in ramshackle monasteries falling into ruins, where life was encrusted with archaic practices. Conscious of all these deficiencies and all this wretchedness, he intrepidly undertook to remedy the state of affairs. It was with this objective that he founded three institutes of Buddhist research: one at Wuchang, which was for a long time his centre of propaganda, where he gave lectures to throngs of voluntary listeners with great success, another at Amoy, and the third in Szechuan, at the frontier of Tibet. This last was with the mission of renovating Tibetan Lamaism, in his eyes tainted with superstition, and of undertaking a critical study of the sacred writings of Lamaism. These institutes put him in contact with the younger elements among the bonzes, who were generally favourable to him and felt the need of instruction and of adaptation to modern times.

His influence was perhaps still greater among the Buddhist laity. To carry out his purpose he created associations designed for intelligent persons in the big cities who desired to deepen their knowledge of the doctrine without indulging in the superstitious practices of the common people, and who desired to participate in social work, such as hospitals, dispensaries, schools, and orphanages. Thoroughly atheistic after the example of the master T'ai Hsü, they strove to bring their social role to the fore with the development of their Buddhist culture. These associations marked a revolution within the Buddhist ranks, for they tended to take away from the bonzes their traditional authority as interpreters of the 'Law' of Buddha.

Finally, T'ai Hsü's intellectual influence also radiated from his writings. Editor of the review *Hai Ch'ao Yin* (海 潮 音) (*The Sound of the Tide*), he campaigned especially for the philosophical school which he had embraced, the school of *wei shih*, or pure idea. Personally very cultivated, he spoke several languages and was well acquainted with Occidental scientific and philosophical theories, with whose aid he tried to give new distinction to his rationalistic and atheistic system.

His efforts encountered a very lively opposition in the ranks of the conservative bonzes who regarded with shame and indignation this rupture with tradition. Moreover, many monasteries in the interior refused hospitality to T'ai Hsü. The leader of this opposition was Yin Kuang, intellectual and spiritual chief of another Buddhist school, the 'Pure Land' sect (also called 'Amidism'). This sect is the most popular in the ranks of Buddhism, and even, one may say, the only one which truly merits the name of religion. Yin Kuang, although well versed in knowledge of the sutras, deems it practically impossible for the common man to save himself by means of meditation and intellectual study, means which are to him inaccessible. For this reason Yin keeps up a voluminous correspondence with young people, and in his writings preaches salvation by faith in the god Amitabha, in Kuan-yin, the goddess who is so popular, and in the bodhisattvas, or 'saints' of Buddhism. He teaches the value of prayer, of creed, of faith, and refuses any adaptation of the doctrine to the conditions of the times. According to him Buddhism holds the highest truth, the absolute truth, and it is therefore fanciful to the point of impiety to seek to harmonize it with modern philosophies or scientific theories.

One sees that there could not be a more complete opposition between the rationalist T'ai Hsü and the pietist Yin Kuang. For the one the doctrine of Buddha is nothing more than a philosophical system, for the other it remains a true religion. Nevertheless, in the words of K. L. Reichelt,[26] the great specialist in modern Buddhism, Yin Kuang the traditionalist represents only the least influential tendency of neo-Buddhism; which is to say, cultivated Buddhist circles are dominated by the atheistic rationalism of T'ai Hsü.

The successor of Ou-Yang Ching-wu in the presidency of the Chinese Academy of Buddhism and the most important of their philosophers, is a layman, Hsiung Shih-li. Like his two predecessors he belongs to the philosophical school of 'mere-ideation', which he has reconstructed on new bases by fusing the classical doctrines of the school with the essential principles of the neo-Confucianism of Wang Yang-ming, and by drawing inspiration from Bergsonian idealism. His system, which has been taught in various universities, was written and published in a definitive form in 1943.

Such in brief have been the vicissitudes of Chinese thought during the last fifty years. One can say that they reflect in all sectors the struggle between traditionalists and progressives, or again, between idealists and materialists; for 'tradition' was rather idealistic on the whole—which is why the champions of tradition have only scorn for the partisans of the Occident. But these champions are everywhere the smaller number, and their complaints awaken fewer and fewer responses.

1. Hu Shih, *Autobiography at the Age of Forty* 四 十 自 述 , p. 99.
2. *Tr. note:* This review was started in 1915 under the title *Ch'ing Nien Tsa Chih* 青 年 雜 誌 (*Youth*). The editor also gave the title in French (*La Jeunesse*). The following year the title became *Hsin Ch'ing Nien* 新 青 年 (*New Youth*).
3. *La Jeunesse Nouvelle*, vol. III, no. 4, June 1, 1917.
4. 'Response to Hu Shih', in Chang Chün-mai, *Science and the Philosophy of Life*, 科 學 與 人 生 觀 , 1925, p. 36.
5. *Essays of Tu-hsiu* 獨 秀 文 存 , vol. I, September 1, 1920.
6. *ibid.*, October 1, 1920.
7. *Essays of Hu Shih*, 2nd Series 胡 適 文 存 二 集 , vol. III, 1924, p. 99.
8. *Essays of Hu Shih*, 1st Series 胡 適 文 存 一 集 , vol. II, 1921, p. 446. (The cited page does not contain this passage.)
9. Fung Yu-lan, *Supplement to the History of Chinese Philosophy* 中 國 哲 學 史 補 , Appendix: 'Philosophy in Contemporary China', 1924.
10. *Essays of Hu Shih*, 1st Series 胡 適 文 存 一 集 , vol. II, 1921, p. 533.
11. Liang Shu-ming, *The Civilizations of Orient and Occident and Their Philosophies* 東 西 文 化 及 其 哲 學 , 1922, p. 202.
12. Cited by Kuo Chan-po, *History of Chinese Thought during the Past Fifty Years* 近 五 十 年 中 國 思 想 史 , 1935, p. 314.
13. *Tr. note:* No reference is given here by author.
14. Cited by Kuo Chan-po, *op. cit.*, p. 322.
15. *China Institute Bulletin*, special number on 'Symposium Science *v.* Philosophy of Life of 1923', article no. 2, 'Reply of Ting Wen-chiang', 1938. (Ting is better known to Westerners as V. K. Ting.)
16. *ibid.*, article no. 3, 'Rejoinder of Chang Chün-mai'.
17. Kuo Chan-po, *op. cit.*, p. 327.
18. *China Institute Bulletin*, issue cited above, article no. 8, 'Science and Philosophy'.
19. Léon Wieger, *Le Flot Montant* (vol. 2 of *La Chine Moderne*, Hien-hien, 1921), p. 72.
20. *ibid.*, p. 72.
21. René Grousset, *Histoire de l'Asie*, t. 2, Paris, 1922, p. 324.

22. H. van Boven, *Histoire de la Littérature Chinoise Moderne*, Peiping, 1946, p. 72.

23. *Tr. note:* The author gives only the Chinese title, 致 知 篇 by which is presumably meant this work.

24. *Tr. note:* Derk Bodde, translator: *A History of Chinese Philosophy.* Volume I: *The Period of the Philosophers (From the beginnings to circa 100 B.C.),* Peiping, Henri Vetch, 1937. (A reprint of this first volume, with corrections and additions, was published in 1952 by Princeton University Press. The second volume, also translated by Bodde, was published in 1953.)

25. *China Christian Year Book, 1936–1937,* Shanghai, p. 67.

26. *Tr. note:* No citation is given here by author.

PART TWO

THE SYSTEMS OF ORIENTAL
DERIVATION

AFTER having surveyed the history of modern ideas in China in broad outline, it is proper to enter into some details in order to give a more precise idea of the principal thinkers and systems, and not to be contented with a too schematic and therefore too vague account. For this purpose it is quite natural to divide our material between authors inspired by Occidental thought, and authors inspired by Oriental ideas. This distinction appears very simple at first glance, but in reality it is not; for one no longer finds thinkers who reason purely in the ancient way, save perhaps the Buddhists. It is a question, then, of unravelling in each of them the predominant tendency. One can say that among all the method is Occidental, but the thought is sometimes more Occidental sometimes more Oriental in allegiance. The difficulty is to judge the exact amount of the respective influences. Be that as it may, one can place in the camp of Oriental thought three groups of thinkers: the Buddhists, the Confucianists, and the vitalists.

The apostle of modernized Buddhism: T'ai Hsü

As for the Buddhists, there is not the shadow of a doubt that their philosophy is purely Oriental in implication, even though they may take some new elements of Occidental science and philosophy to integrate into their system. Their principal theoretician, T'ai Hsü, whose social and intellectual role we are going to retrace, was a very cultivated man, different from the traditional bonzes, who knew nothing other than their sutras. As we have seen, he was given the mission of renovating Buddhism in his own country; but he was also a very active propagandist abroad. He participated in numerous congresses, not only in the countries bordering China, such as

45

Japan, the Philippines, the East Indies, and Ceylon, but even in Europe and America. In 1928 he gave a series of lectures in Paris, Frankfort, Berlin, London and New York. He planned the creation of a world-wide Institute of Buddhism, with headquarters in China and branches in all countries, but was not able to accomplish this plan. Here is how he himself characterized the main features of his work: 'Not long since most people regarded Buddhism as a polytheistic religion with superstitious rites; but now this conception begins to be shaken. Not long since the Sacred Books were only studied by hermits in the mountains or by bonzes in the pagodas (*sic*); but now well educated people study them in common. Not long since only the monasteries were considered as organs of Buddhism; but now there are propaganda circles, conferences and cultural societies, on the provincial level as well as on the national plane. Not long since the Buddhist Law had no relation to the ways and customs of the country; but now it is the norm which attracts the throngs to Buddhism. Not long since to practice Buddhism was equivalent to leading a solitary life, shut up, secluded from society; now, on the contrary, Buddhism goes before the people and places itself at the service of human life.'[1]

The texts of his lectures were published by his disciples in books and small propaganda tracts. But he himself wrote a good number of works, of which the principal one is *The True Realism* (真現 實論), published in its entirety only in 1940. He seeks to establish the rational doctrine of his system—the school of 'pure ideation'—by means of scientific facts. The metaphysics which he expounds is based on the Buddhist theory of knowledge, according to which the only true reality is not the world of appearances, but the world of laws, the subject of knowledge in the mind, 'alaya'. This is always an unstable state, for it is perpetually influenced by the perceptions and impression arising from external appearances. In seeking to know the 'noumenon', the 'law', one advances along the way of virtue which conducts one to the illumination, the perfect intuition of nirvana, partially attained by the saints or bodhisattvas, and completely attained by the Buddha. This effort to penetrate the ultimate reality of all being does not postulate the necessity of a God. Buddhism does not adore gods; it is resolutely atheistic. Although it honours Buddha and the bodhisattvas, these are purely commemorative titles, 'as we raise statues to those who have deserved them from their country', in order to remember the heroes who have arrived partially or totally at 'illumination'. The worship rendered by the people to these heroes is pure superstition, regrettable error. 'Owing to the fact that many people burn incense and candles, erect idols, and try to obtain good luck,' he says, 'a great number of educated moderns do not realize that Buddhism is atheistic, that the Buddha is only our leader, our precursor, our master. We respect him because he leads us towards the enlightenment inherent in our own nature and helps us to become Buddha. Gods and spirits represent only one of six phases of life; they are themselves deserving of pity and have need of salvation. Thus, then, the great design of Buddhism is to dissipate ignorance and to bring enlightenment. . . . The Chinese term for Buddha, "Fo", signifies "illumination". All men have a nature capable of becoming "illumined"; all could, in other words, become Buddha. He who has arrived at a true comprehension of man and the universe can be called "illumined". Buddha is neither a Creator nor a God who controls human nature: he is only a man who has attained to total enlightenment in the universe.'[2]

Then T'ai Hsü analyses the content of the concept 'illumination' and boils it down to four great principles: the eternity of the flux of being, the origin of being in the consciousness, negation of the self, and negation of the objective existence of the universe. These four truths are easier to expound than to realize: they are practically beyond the grasp of the average man. There is a method to follow in order to arrive at grasping untuitively the ultimate reality of the universe. 'Those who are near to illumination should reveal the method by which Buddhahood can be attained. There are three paths: the first consists of developing self-control; the second is mental concentration; the third is knowledge, derived from instruction, from thought, and from strict mental discipline.'[3] The first path is put into practice by the humble classes, the faithful of the cult of Amitabha. Sometimes even T'ai Hsü, who disapproves of these forms of worship as being tainted with superstition, does not disdain to participate in them, because he recognizes them as necessary practices in the salvation of the ignorant. However, the faithful cannot arrive at total illumination by this path; by it, they may only attain to the 'Paradise of the West', which is an intermediate stage bringing them nearer to nirvana. To more cultivated people T'ai Hsü counsels the more difficult but more rapid path of meditation.

Such are the main points of his doctrine. But he does not occupy himself exclusively with instruction, with teaching the means conducive to illumination. On occasion he puts his readers on guard against modern doctrines or theories which he thinks contrary to his faith. In 1927, at the time when Communism began to become a national movement, he wrote a work entitled *A View of the History of Liberty* (自 由 史 觀), in which he denounced the evils of all dogmatisms and religions, as well as imperialism and communism. Then he explained succinctly the essentials of Buddhism and showed that it alone correctly understands liberty.

A neo-Buddhist eclectic: Hsiung Shih-li

T'ai Hsü died suddenly in 1947, taken prematurely by an illness; he was not yet sixty. He had been a classical exponent of the *wei shih* system, but without great originality, according to his critics. One cannot say the same about Hsiung Shih-li, who proves to be much more individualistic and less traditional in his work, *New Exposition of [the Treatise on] Pure Idea* (新 唯 識 論) (1944). Not long before a certain Chou Pao-chang had already attempted to interpret the system by basing himself on the theories of Alfred North Whitehead. This he did in an essay entitled *A New Interpretation of the Wei-shih School*.[4] Hsiung Shih-li undertakes to reconstruct the system with the aid of Wang Yang-ming and Bergson. The alliance of Wang Yang-ming and Buddhism is not a new fact in the history of Chinese philosophy. Wang Yang-ming and neo-Confucianism were a product of Buddhist idealism and Confucian idealism, and there is an obvious correlation, a relationship of spirit and even of nature, between the two idealisms.

Here is how Hsiung Shih-li establishes his system. Being in itself is immaterial, absolute, eternal, whole, pure, strong. Now human nature enjoys the same prerogatives as Being in itself. This substance in itself is the whole of nature; it dominates the ego as it dominates all beings, the subject as well as the object. Integrated in individual natures, the said substance at one and the same time includes the pure knowledge of reason and the love of goodness in Confucianism. 'Goodness is nature; that is to say, the common substance of ego-subject and beings-objects.'[5] But it is necessary to distinguish between this nature and its activities. Nature in itself is eternal, but not its activities, such as thoughts, volitions, and sensations, which form the subject matter of psychology. 'The spirit as to its nature is anterior; as to its activity, that is posterior.'[6] The activity of nature manifests matter as opposed to spirit. Spirit and matter are not two beings, but two contrary aspects of a substantial whole. Hereby the author believes he has done away with pure idealism and pure materialism, which he declares eternally inseparable since they constitute two aspects of a whole. Nevertheless, before the world was made manifest, before one could speak of psychological phenomena, there was already a pre-existent obscure and blind spirit. 'Although spirit manifests itself more and more in the state of organic matter, one cannot doubt that there was a spirit, a hidden active force, before the advent of organic matter.'[7] From this he draws his conclusion as to the existence of a spirit or soul of the world: 'Each being possesses a spirit, which is the soul of the world; then the soul of the world is only the spirit of particular beings.'[8] Is this pantheism? No, the author knows that pantheistic doctrines are very unmodish in our day, and are considered anti-scientific. So he thinks he can avoid the reproach of pantheism by denying to spirit united with matter the quality of individual, autonomous, personal entity. For him the spirit underlying the subjective ego as well as the objective world is only an aspect of the manifestation of substance in itself—the Kantian noumenon.

Does not such an impersonal substance court the danger of being nothing more than a concept, devoid of all reality? No, for the activities of spirit, the flow of evolution, give evidence of the reality of this spirit; for spirit and its activities are inseparable. This spiritual substance is only revealed by evolution, for substance and movement are indissolubly united; there is no substance aside from movement or movement without substance. This substance in itself is unknow-able, indescribable, but we can perceive its manifestations, we can describe its activities. The universe is, then, only a process of constant transformations, without any distinction between the domain of subjective consciousness and the objective material world, between spirit and matter, between the one and the many. Neither material elements nor spiritual elements have any real nature in themselves. Only unlimited evolution is real. As such it is life, vital energy, existing and sufficing unto itself, the great current of production and reproduction of the universe which cannot be perceived except by intuition.

These last words obviously bear the impress of Bergsonism, as we have remarked above. On the whole, Hsiung Shih-li does not have the same preoccupations as T'ai Hsü. He does not pose as anything other than a philosopher, a theoretician of knowledge, and does not have the philosophical bonze's purpose of salvation. Also he is bolder with regard to his system and influenced to a larger extent by non-Buddhist philosophies. Hence he is more original. He makes much use of the ideas of Wang Yang-ming, just as those ideas were themselves largely suggested by Buddhist idealism.

We are thus brought quite naturally to the study of the recent representatives of Confucianism; for, despite all the attacks of the 'Occidentalists', or 'progressives', Confucian thought is still lively—livelier than Buddhist thought with its special concepts which are intelligible only to specialists.

Modern Confucian thought is divided into two rather opposing tendencies: the positivistic rationalism of Chu Hsi extolled by Fung Yu-lan, and the intuitive, immanentistic idealism of Wang Yang-ming upheld by Ho Lin and others.

Positivistic neo-Confucianism: Fung Yu-lan

Fung Yu-lan is the highest philosophical authority in China at the present time. He has held this position since 1931, by the publication of the first volume of his *History of Chinese Philosophy* (中 國 哲 學 史),[9] which outclassed all the other treatises of the same type, including that of Hu Shih. It has not yet been surpassed. But he did not undertake exposition of his own system until the end of 1939. In this connection his most important work is *New Li Hsüeh* (新 理 學), which contains the metaphysical principles of which he makes particular applications to morals, sociology, etc.

The central concept of the Cheng-Chu school of neo-Confucianism was *li* (王里), Reason, the Norm, which exists eternally in itself and is not altered by its actualization in beings. Even though it be extra-temporal and extra-spatial, the Norm must rule the World. The universe is only the Norm actualized, revealed; thus the norm of a being is the ideal law of this being. The whole of these actualized norms is called the Great One, the Ultimate One. In order to pass to being, an entity requires also another principle, the vital and material principle, or *ch'i* (氣). Every being is modelled on its formal principle, *li*, and on its material principle, *ch'i*. When the formal principle is actualized, it is dynamic, the generator of movement; whereas *ch'i* is passive and static. This modality is expressed by the two concepts of ancient philosophy, *yin* (陰) and *yang* (陽); *yin* is destroyer and *yang* is creator. They are purely logical (*sic*). Their activity produces the perpetual flux, the constant evolution in the course of transformation. This gradual evolution regularly embraces all beings. When an entity is actualized in accord with its 'norm', its nature is realized and its mission performed. From the logical point of view nature is neither good nor bad; but from the point of view of actuality it is good, since it always follows the 'norm' to some degree. From the practical point of view, however, when an entity does not reach a higher degree of norm, it is called bad. Moral badness is thus a 'failure to develop its own behaviour', its nature. If the nature, on the other hand, follows the norm completely, then the nature and the norm are integrally realized. To fulfil his mission, to conform to the norm, man has to expand his knowledge, for the content of the norm can only be known by systematic and objective study—whence the utility of induction and the experimental method. By analysing actualized beings, one can penetrate the domain of reality, and by that, the domain of truth. When one considers things correctly, he sees them 'from the point of view of Heaven'; when he considers the myriads of beings as a unity, he is in accord with *jen* (仁), or the ideal good, and puts himself into the transcendental world.

In expounding these theories Fung Yu-lan corrects the fundamental concepts of neo-Confucianism and puts the Norm out beyond beings, instead of leaving it immersed in the interior of reality. This is Fung's great revolution. The neo-Confucianists had claimed, indeed, that the norm was in things, and that it could not be beyond them. Fung has broken with this sort of immanentism, and adopted transcendentalism. Likewise he has developed the logical side, whereas the ancients had favoured the practical and moral side. In order to set up his system he relies constantly on Chu Hsi, whom he cites at every step; but he is influenced also by a Taoist philosopher, Kuo Hsiang, one of the principal commentators of Chuang Tzu. (It should be borne in mind now, that the Taoist school represents the materialistic side of Chinese speculation.) Fung rarely draws on Wang Yang-ming and hardly cites him except to attack him; which is to say that the general tendency of his philosophy is positivistic.

Fung Yu-lan also makes use of the Taoist idea of the *tao* (道), while giving his own interpretation to this word. He compares it with his Norm, and when one rereads the first lines of the *Tao Te Ching* (道 德 經) of Lao Tzu, one is struck by the analogy between this *tao* and the *li* of Fung Yu-lan. 'The Power which can be defined is not the eternal Power; the name by which it can be named is not its eternal name. When nameless, it is the origin of the universe . . .; when it has a name, it is the genetrix (mother) of all things. Therefore (only he who is) ever passionless may behold its mystery. (He who is) ever subject to his passions may (only) see its external manifestations. These two things (i.e. the mysterious or immaterial, and the manifestation, or material) differ in name, but are the same in origin. Their unity is a deep, a deep of deeps, it is the portal of all mystery.'[10] This impersonal or manifested *tao* seems clearly to have inspired more than one modern thinker besides Fung Yu-lan, even though the words may differ a little.

Be that as it may, this transcendental *li* or *tao*, is it not finally equivalent to a personal or impersonal God? For Fung, in no way: neither monotheism nor pantheism are admissible. 'We cannot admit the existence of a cosmic soul. For us, the universe is only a general term, a *universal*; it does not call for a real structure necessitating a soul. Only the superior animals have a soul. The existence of a cosmic spirit is impossible in our system. From this point of view we sympathize with materialism.'[11]

Many people, however, practise a religion and believe in a real God, and that helps them to get beyond themselves, giving them at least the illusion of attaining an unattainable. The surroundings and circumstances help them to create this psychological state—the majesty of temples, the beauty of ceremonies, the harmony of chants. But it is only illusion, a false consolation. One cannot admit the existence of a Norm or Reason beyond beings except in the sense of a term which is true 'logically', not true 'really'. But to seek to transcend sensible experience must be the aim of all life, for thereby one tends towards the perfection of his norm. In order to reach this transcendence, one can choose between two paths, that of the genius and that of the sage. The man of talent, the genius, discovers all at once, in a sudden illumination, in an intuitive flash, a truth, scientific, philosophical, etc., and this furtive glimpse which he casts beyond the present world is called 'creation'. It is evident that this process is not available to everyone. Happily there is another method of transcending experience which is accessible to all: that is the practice of 'wisdom'. The sage penetrates into the holy city of 'wisdom' by means of knowledge, by philosophical activity (not 'science'), by the analysis of beings, which teaches him to know the real, and then the true logic. Finally this culminates in moral activity. In the first stage, that of science, he learns to go beyond experience: in the second, that of moral practice, he learns to go beyond the egoistical self. One discovers the traces of Reason or the transcendental Norm in material beings, and not in the human heart as was asserted by Wang Yang-ming. 'Without moral activity we could not pass beyond the egoistical self. Now the true character of moral activity is to go beyond the egoistical self. It is then in moral or social activity that man can attain the higher regions of the surpassing of self.'[12] Such is the difference between man and animal. When man has attained to this stage, he has thereby a conscience and uses it; he attains happiness, and by that he exercises a real influence on the universe. In this sense one can call him 'the soul of the world'.

Idealistic neo-Confucianism: Ho Lin

This Confucian rationalism, despite the high authority of Fung Yu-lan, and despite the official esteem which it has enjoyed during the centuries, yet does not seem to us to express the dominant tendency among Confucian thinkers. The greater number seems to us still to follow the interpretation of Wang Yang-ming. Among all the disciples of the great idealist thinker, Ho Lin may be considered the most eminent, although his authority is not comparable to that of Fung Yu-lan. Professor of philosophy at the University of Peking, Ho Lin is one of the best representatives of Sino-Occidental idealism. He studied in Germany, where he specialized in the study of Hegel, but in China he is best known for his commentaries on Wang Yang-ming and Sun Yat-sen, who had taken it upon himself to modify an essential formula of Wang Yang-ming. Responding to an address by Chiang Kai-shek, Ho Lin composed a small book on the question of *knowledge* and *action*, in order to show that the points of view of Sun and Wang are not very different at bottom, that they are only two aspects of the same truth. Wang Yang-ming advocated the union of knowledge and action, while according the pre-eminence to action. He especially had in mind a moral point of view: 'True knowledge is for action; without action one could not speak of knowledge.'[13] Besides, they perfectly interpenetrate each other: 'Knowledge, in so far as it is true, sincere, is already action; action, in so far as it is enlightened, is already knowledge.'[14] Sun Yat-sen was taken with this theory and applied it to the political domain; only he insisted on the difficulty of knowing. While doing the same, Ho Lin enunciated an axiom of universal import, as much in the line of neo-Confucianism as in the Occidental tradition of Plato, Aristotle, Kant, and Hegel. The dream of this author is to unite these two philosophies, to enliven them, the one by the other, for they are 'the two greatest philosophies of the world'. He concludes that the commentary of Chiang Kai-shek adds a new point of view, which solves the problem: it is in action that one finds true knowledge, not in speculative truth.

Thus far Ho Lin has published only fragmentary studies, essays, and criticisms, not any systematic work. We are assured, however, that he will soon publish the main points of his metaphysics. Be that as it may, it is easy to review the principal questions with which he is preoccupied, according to collections of his studies.

He dwells above all on moral and cultural problems. Resolutely the idealist, he recommends the cult of heroes as the foundation of education. In education to neglect the cult of heroes amounts to neglecting the formation of personality and character, and it devolves

into a purely commercial, mechanical enterprise. This depersonaliza-
tion renders classes dreary, banal, dry and lifeless. There lies one of
the truly great dangers of education in China.[15] This cult of heroes
must eventuate in developing in man the understanding of the
struggle to subdue blind reality and to triumph over the oppressions
which hinder the happiness of modern man. In case of failure he
must not be discouraged, but persevere—whence the importance of
optimism as an attitude of life. It is necessary to cultivate confidence
in oneself and in others, but 'the optimistic attitude depends on the
ideal'.[16] Indeed, if exterior action is not joined to interior virtue,
the material and economic prosperity of the nation cannot rest on
solid bases. 'A progress based on a mere accumulation of money or
riches, which did not result in striving after wisdom and virtue,
would not in the end be a real economic value.'[17]

Along with the creed of action it is necessary to develop the taste
for study, for culture. Study differentiates man from animal, the
civilized from the savage. By study we come into contact with the
most eminent minds of all times, we absorb the spiritual heritage
of the past and the marrow of modern thought; and this thought,
which is the fruit of so much work, reflection, discussion and
reading, is given to us crystallized and condensed, and is part of our
flesh and blood every moment. 'Yes, truly, by study man has a holy
power.'[18] Theoretical, even conceptual knowledge is indispensable
today: it is the necessary preparation for modern creation. 'If the
Chinese want to enter by the door of science, to penetrate into the
palace of technique, they should modify their traditional practical
attitude of adoration of matter and military force, and recognize
the true value of theory. To begin with, they should take account
of the power of concepts, especially of speculative concepts.'[19] The
author is so imbued with the importance of theoretical knowledge,
of culture, that he makes it the principal subject of his recent book
Culture and Life (文 化 與 人 生) (1947), as well as of his
preceding work, *A Brief Exposition of Idealism* (近 代 唯 心
論 簡 釋) published in 1942.

To sum up: Ho Lin's thought has no frontiers; he draws as much
on Occidental systems as on traditional Chinese philosophy. The
author himself states in the preface to *Culture and Life*: 'My judg-
ments, my opinions, bring together especially Chinese Confucianist

thought and that of Kant, Fichte, and Hegel, the representatives of Occidental idealism.' In other words, German idealism and Confucian idealism are his inspirations: the one completes the other. He desires to inaugurate a philosophical system which would be made up of a synthesis of Socrates, Plato, Aristotle, Kant and Hegel with Confucius, Mencius, Chu Hsi and Wang Yang-ming. The syncretism thus obtained would revitalize Confucian thought and give it a new scope.

One sees that Ho Lin is rather difficult to catalogue in one camp or the other. If we prefer to place him among the 'Orientalists', it is because of his general view and his writings on Wang Yang-ming. Ma I-fu, associate professor at the Institute of Life Renovation, is more definitely Confucian in the whole of his thought. In *Conversations at T'ai Ho* (泰 和 會 語), *Conversations at I Shan* (宜 山 會 語), and *The General Meaning of the Four Books* (四 書 大 義), he has synthesized and explained the doctrine of the four neo-Confucian Canons, the *Analects of Confucius*, the *Great Learning*, the *Doctrine of the Mean* and *Mencius*. Thus he shows himself to be an adept of the original, traditional Confucianism, but he does not seek to explain it by means of Buddhist or Taoist thought, as some others have done. He possesses a background of poetry, rites and metaphysics, the three branches of knowledge necessary to every orthodox Confucian. At the beginning he follows the interpretation of Chu Hsi, but later he draws nearer to Wang Yang-ming.

The problem which has principally concerned him is that of civilization. According to him culture is summed up in six arts, the six arts held in honour by Confucianism. That, as he puts it, means to know poetry, literature, rites, music, history and etiquette. These six arts represent the spiritual activity of every man. Even Occidental culture can be comprised within this cultural system of the six arts; for it contains, in fact, the same values of goodness, beauty and truth, poetry and literature corresponding to goodness, rites and music to beauty, history and etiquette to truth.[20] These six sections of culture have their origin in the human heart, and not in material conditions. Thus culture is in essence spiritual from the start. So long as the human heart exists, civilization cannot perish. This expresses the universal value of Confucianism, of traditional

Chinese culture. 'If humanity wishes to issue forth from darkness and advance towards the light, it has no other way.'[21]

Confucianism is not limited to the few authors whose essential theses we have analysed. It would be necessary to add many other names of the first rank, such as Chang Chün-mai, Liang Shu-ming, etc., whom we have already mentioned earlier.

The philosophy of tridemism: Sun Yat-sen, Chiang K'ai-shek

There remains a third group of thinkers greatly influenced by Confucianism, and so included among the philosophers of national derivation. These are the theoreticians of the Nationalist Party, Sun Yat-sen and Chiang K'ai-shek for political and economic doctrine, and Ch'en Li-fu for the metaphysical foundation.

Sun Yat-sen was, as everyone knows, the principal actor of the revolution of 1911 which overthrew the Empire in favour of a republic, whence his appellation, 'Father of the Country'. His economic, political, and social principles have been expounded in his famous book, much commentated upon, *The Three Principles of the People*, or *Tridemism* (三 民 主 義), a collection of lectures delivered at Canton in 1924. It does not enter into our subject to explain the essential ideas of that work. What interests us here about the theories of Sun Yat-sen is their ideological foundation. As for political party techniques, his ideas were borrowed from the great economists and politicians of the Occident; but the underlying thought on which they rest derives from the Confucian tradition.

Sun Yat-sen retains two elements of that tradition in particular, the ideal of the great harmony, and consciousness of the problem of the relation between knowledge and action. Confucius had developed a Utopian ideal of peace and universal brotherhood by the practice of *jen* 仁 , the Confucian virtue *par excellence*, equivalent to our concepts of humanity, brotherhood, and love among men. This ideal was taken up again and delineated by K'ang Yu-wei, who, as we have seen, made it the subject of a special book (*Ta T'ung Shu* 大 同 書). In his turn Sun Yat-sen was haunted by the yearning for an ultimate universal peace founded upon a sense of brotherhood which would unite the peoples of the entire world. He wanted to procure the welfare of his people as of other peoples; he wanted to give them peace within and without—a desire all the more ardent in him, as the nation became more and more disordered. The Confucianist aspiration was already 'socialism' before the word was invented.

The second Confucianist element on which Sun Yat-sen based himself in order to try to instil a new spirit into the people, was the relation between knowledge and action. Wang Yang-ming, as we have stated earlier, had strongly insisted on the synthesis of knowledge and action, this in order to remedy a grave defect among the *literati*. Those men were so imbued with the importance of culture, of knowledge, that they rather neglected action. Hence Sun Yat-sen: 'As soon as you know, act. If you do nothing, what good is your knowledge to you? It will lose all significance: not to act, is not to know.'[22] On the very morrow of his political triumphs of 1911, after having overthrown the Empire and seen himself proclaimed the first President of the Chinese Republic, Sun Yat-sen experienced bitter disillusionment in the pursuit of his dreams. He felt himself so badly supported that he offered his resignation. Becoming an ordinary citizen again, he reflected on the causes of his failure and was persuaded that the root of the difficulty was in ignorance, rather than in the incapacity to act. That is why he launched a campaign to reform the popular error concerning knowledge and action: 'I champion the doctrines of Wang Yang-ming, who advocated the union of action and knowledge. To know and to act are but one. The old tradition is false. It is opposed to the truth. I understand the reasons for China's weakness. If our people do not act, it is because they are completely ignorant.'[23] In short Sun emphasizes the difficulty of knowledge, thus taking a different view from Wang Yang-ming. But conditions have changed. That which could be psychologically exact in the time of Wang Yang-ming, is not so today. 'Even if the teaching of Wang Yang-ming contributed to the awakening of Japan,' as many people believe, Sun affirms that this teaching was more disastrous than useful to the Chinese people. He gives a series of ten examples to prove the difficulty of knowledge and the easiness of action. Demonstration of this thesis is the object of a book which he published in 1918 under the title *On Psychological Reconstruction* (心 理 建 設 論), a book which had many repercussions and was afterwards studied and commentated on by the philosophers and theoreticians of the Kuomintang. The author expected much of this campaign of ideas: 'The Chinese today, at least most of them, despise knowledge and admire action. This tendency is unfortunate. In our age of science we have come to honour knowledge as much as action... I deem it my duty to deliver the minds of my countrymen from this preconceived idea that 'to know is easy and to act difficult', to bring them, by repeated explanations and arguments, to think that 'action is easy and knowledge hard'. I hope that they will abandon this false dogma which may seem correct at first view, but which is none the less an error. If I succeed, the future of China will be great.'[24]

The successor of Sun Yat-sen, Chiang K'ai-shek, retained this new theory that 'action is easy and knowledge hard', but still derived from it a doctrine of action. While he was still only the director of the Whampoa Military Academy, he commented to the cadets on many occasions on the motto of Wang Yang-ming and the correction given it by Sun Yat-sen. He even made it the foundation of his oral and written teaching. 'In the universe without any regard to the age or the circumstances there is but one word, action, and action is creator. Thus the idea that to know is difficult and that action is easy forms the centre of our philosophy of life. In other words, we have to consider the philosophy of action as our philosophy of life.'[25] In his book, *China's Destiny* (中 國 之 命 運), published in March 1943, Chiang returns to this teaching of Sun Yat-sen, approves it and makes it his own. He wants to imbue his compatriots with this spirit of action, which seems to him the key to the whole psychological reconstruction of the nation: 'Our fellow citizens should actively become creators; they should take the initiative and transform their cold lethargy into a warm enthusiasm for progress. In particular they must change their present attitude of passivity and depression into positive, determined, audacious action.'[26]

Besides this propaganda in favour of action in which he takes without so saying the opposite attitude to Sun Yat-sen, practically returning to Wang Yang-ming, Chiang K'ai-shek has also worked to restore the ancient ideals of the Confucian ethic. When he launched the New Life Movement on February 15, 1934, it was as we have seen for the purpose of restoring a national spirit to China by reviving the great virtues of Confucianism, reason, rectitude, honour, and justice. In *China's Destiny* he proclaims anew the first necessity in the strengthening of the nation. This he calls ethical reconstruction. He considers this philosophy of life, characteristic of China, as the highest expression of morals which exists in the world: 'China's own philosophy, developed by Confucius, amplified and propagated by Mencius, and later explained by the *literati* of the Han Dynasty, is automatically a sublime system, superior to all other philosophies in the world. . . . The glories and the design of the ancient Chinese doctrines have never been equalled among today's Occidental Powers.'[27]

Response to this vigorous campaign by the Chief of State in favour of Confucianism was evinced not only in the quite rapid extension of the New Life Movement, but also in the personal initiative of certain provincial governors, and in the writings and discourses of statesmen like Wang Ching-wei. The latter, both before and after his passing over to co-operation with the Japanese, warmly sang the praises of Confucius and his culture. In Kwangtung Governor-General Chen Chi-tang, in Honan General Ho Chien, in North China General Sung Che-yuan, were warm apostles of Confucianism. They established schools to bring the study of the Confucian Classics back into favour. The aim of this resurrection of Confucianism, which dates from 1934, was to restore to the people an ideology, so as to battle against the theories of materialism and class strife.

The metaphysics of tridemism: the vitalism of Ch'en Li-fu

During the same period another politician, Ch'en Li-fu, gave a series of lectures which were later brought together in a book, in which he elaborated a new system of philosophy called 'vitalism' furnishing a metaphysical foundation for tridemism.

His point of departure was a phrase of Sun Yat-sen's expressed thus: 'Life is the centre of the world.' Stressing this concept of 'life', Ch'en Li-fu set out to keep the exact balance between idealism and materialism, and in that way to steer clear of the drawbacks of monism, whether idealistic or materialistic, and of dualism. Hence the name of vitalism which he gives to his system. He aspires to effect a synthesis between idealism and materialism in the transcendent; for, he notes, 'in the universe, there is no being entirely formed from spirit or entirely buried in matter. Not only do absolute spirit and pure matter not exist, but also matter and spirit are essentially relative terms, offering between them only a difference in degree. Indeed spirit and matter, from the fact of the substantial unity constituting their being—the primitive monad of all beings—are distinguished only by free mobility or stable immobility; they are then correlative.'[28] Here is the basic principle upon which his whole system rests. One cannot forbear to remark that the author takes a singular way of refuting materialism, the ultimate goal of his endeavour. Far from getting rid of it, he only gives it a helping hand from the start, since in his view, the only difference between beings is a smaller or larger dose of spirit among the three kingdoms of nature, the animal, vegetable, and mineral. There is even a gradation within each species, for certain species form the bridge from one kingdom to another. Thus coral is cited as forming the intermediary link between mineral and vegetable.

The monad, which is the smallest cosmic unity possible metaphysically—what is called electron or cell or atom—consists of a static quality, matter, and a dynamic force, spirit. The multiplicity of entities and species comes from the variable number of monads or their combinations in the interior of an entity. All these entities have life to one degree or another, even the minerals, since they are endowed with spiritual energy and material substance. All are faced with the struggle for existence, and this struggle is the principle of worldly evolution, of incessant progress.

Having arrived at the stage of the monad 'man', the author studies the exercise of the human faculties on four planes of action: autonomy or free will, growth, power of resistance, and the faculty of transmitting life. Through these diverse activities man evolves and progresses all down through history. This progress starts with existence, the raw state of existence that one can consider as Truth, traverses the stage of Goodness, or improved existence, and culminates in the stage of Beauty, in which existence is the most perfect possible, being in possession of all the last refinements. The meaning and value of life lies in the effort to beautify it. Before arriving at the ideal state, humanity must go through seven stages. Having attained to the perfect, ultimate stage, man, thanks to the spirit of co-operation, trust, and mutual love, gives the best that he has, and takes what he wishes according to his needs. Having constantly in mind the idea of existence and collective progress, men live to a standard of absolute equality, in perfect concord, without distinction of race, class, or sex. Life is worthy to be called beautiful and harmonious only in such a community. This is the Confucian ideal of universal concord, and Ch'en Li-fu intends by upholding it to defeat the Marxist dream of the final communist society.

In the pursuit of this ideal society the Orient and Occident vie ardently, but in a different manner. Chinese civilization puts the emphasis on the spiritual phase of life, and more especially on the virtues necessary to the relations between men, such as benevolence, fidelity, and sincerity; whereas Occidental civilization lays stress on the material phase—whence its efforts and its success in scientific discoveries. The synthesis of these two civilizations is indispensable to the creation of the international society of the Great Concord. The one will furnish the material element and the other the spiritual element. 'We believe', says the author, 'that humanity, in order to attain to this ideal world of universal concord, must adopt the spiritual characteristics of Chinese civilization, and that we Chinese must develop and augment in ourselves these spiritual elements in order to create the civilization with which to endow humanity.'[29]

Several authors have tried to exploit this new metaphysic, but on the whole it has not elicited any great response. It marks an attempt to unite Confucianism and science, the ancient conception of the Great Concord with the socialistic ideal of a dream-society. It is above all a reaction against the rise of the Marxist philosophy within the ranks of the Chinese intelligentsia. While the Kuomintang armies made a last effort to crush the Communist State in Kiangsi, politicians and military governors also undertook an ideological offensive to restore the Confucian ideal to favour. The year 1934 saw (1) the Communist armies leave Kiangsi to undertake the famous Long March which resulted in the formation of a new Communist State in the north of Shensi, (2) Chiang K'ai-shek inaugurating the New Life Movement, (3) General Ho Chien establishing Confucianist schools in Hunan, and (4) the philosopher Chang Tung-sun publishing a book of philosophical essays criticizing Marxism. The lectures of Ch'en Li-fu to the students of the School of Political Science in

Nanking certainly followed a studied plan; so that it was not by chance that a collection of these lectures entitled *Vitalism* (唯生論) appeared in the same year.

Briefly, to sum up in a few lines this account of the systems which are more obviously of Oriental derivation, it must be said that Confucianism still remains a force, the greatest spiritual force of China, and that Buddhism, second in favour, is trying to climb back up from its decadence by deepening its philosophy and attempting to harmonize it with science and with Occidental thought. Bygone authors of antiquity have also been studied a great deal—the Taoists Lao Tzu and Chuang Tzu for their worship of Nature, Mo Ti for his theories of universal love and his pragmatic, utilitarian elements, Han Fei Tzu for his conception of government by law, and Wang Ch'ung and Wang An-shih for their socialist ideas.[30] But none of these has inspired the thinkers of the period in a profound enough way to give birth to syncretist systems in which the old ideas would be the predominant elements.

The greatest part of opinion is no longer being led by the ancient sages of China; it has resolutely turned towards Occidental theories. Our task is now to establish this.

1. *T'ai Hsü's Discourses* 太虛演說集 , vol. I, 1932, p. 209.
2. T'ai Hsü, *The A.B.C. of Buddhism* 佛學 A.B.C., p. 67. *Tr. note:* This title is not listed in the Bibliography. The author has not indicated whether or not all of the above quoted material is taken from this same source.
3. *ibid.*, p. 70.
4. *Tr. note:* The author does not give Chinese characters for either this man or his book, nor is he listed in the Bibliography.
5. Ho Lin, *Contemporary Chinese Philosophy* 當代中國哲學 , 1941, p. 14.
6. *loc. cit.*
7. *ibid.*, p. 15.

8. *loc. cit.*

9. *Tr. note:* See above, Part One, note 24.

10. W. E. Soothill, *The Three Religions of China*, London, 3rd ed., 1913, pp. 47–8.

11. *New Li Hsüeh* 新 理 學 , p. 161.

12. *ibid.*, p. 303.

13. Wang Tch'ang-tche, *La Philosophie Morale de Wang Yang-ming* (*Variétés Sinologiques*, no. 63), Shanghai, 1936, p. 83.

14. *loc. cit.*

15. Ho Lin, *Culture and Life* 文 化 與 人 生 , 1947, p. 142. *Tr. note:* There is no initial quotation mark in the text. This work is not listed in the Bibliography.

16. *ibid.*, p. 165.

17. *ibid.*, p. 226.

18. *ibid.*, p. 261.

19. *ibid.*, p. 246.

20. *Tr. note:* There is obviously some confusion in the foregoing, presumably some proof-reading error: note, for example, the otiose repetition in 'ritual' and 'etiquette'. The term 'Lui I' (the Six Arts) originally denoted the six branches of Eastern-Chou education for nobles, but in Han times the term came to be a common expression for six Confucianist compendia, these compendia being in process of becoming canonical scriptures: the *Poems* (or *Songs*), the *Historical Writings* (or *Documents*), the *Rituals*, the *Music* (and Ritual Dances), the *Changes*, and the *Spring-and-Autumn Annals* (of Lu State). According to Ho Lin in the work cited (see note 5), 'Among the Six Arts [i.e. Scriptures] the *Poems* and the *Historical Writings* appertain to goodness, the *Rituals* and the *Music* appertain to beauty, and the *Changes* and the *Spring-and-Autumn* appertain to truth.' The neo-Confucians while exalting 'the Four Books' to prime canonical status in no sense de-canonized the other Scriptures.

21. Ho Lin, *Contemporary Chinese Philosophy* 當 代 中 國 哲 學 , 1941, p. 17.

22. Sun Yat-sen, *Souvenirs d'un Revolutionnaire Chinois*, Paris, 1933, p. 90.

23. *ibid.*, Preface, p. 13.

24. *ibid.*, p. 102.

25. Cited by Hollington K. Tong, *Chiang K'ai-shek: Soldier and Statesman* (authorized biography), Shanghai, 1937, vol. II, p. 604.

26. Chiang K'ai-shek, *China's Destiny* 中 國 之 命 運 , 1943, p. 163.
27. *ibid.*, p. 16.
28. Ch'en Li-fu, *Vitalism* 唯 生 論 , 1934, p. 29.
29. Ch'en Li-fu, *The Origin of Life* 生 之 原 理 , 1944, p. 307. *Tr. note:* This is the quotation as the author has given it, although it does not illustrate the sentence immediately preceding, as it does not give the other half of the equation: the material elements of Occidental civilization.
30. *Tr. note:* Both here and in the Bibliography Wang Ch'ung is stated to have espoused socialistic ideas, so the translator has not changed the text. However, he has ventured to replace the name of Kung-sun Lung immediately above with that of Han Fei Tzu, since it is obvious that this was a slip of the author's pen.

PART THREE

THE SYSTEMS OF OCCIDENTAL
DERIVATION

THE immense majority of the intellectuals profess Comte's axiom on the three ages of mankind. Man, after having traversed the theological and philosophical ages, finally reaches the scientific age. Consequently all philosophy which seeks to survive must be scientific philosophy. That is why it is necessary to turn towards the more logical Occidental systems, and, drawing more inspiration from scientific theories, cease to use some elements of the traditional Chinese systems.

In classifying the principal thinkers who have been moved by this spirit, we shall adopt the customary division into metaphysicians, logicians, moralists and aestheticians. Doubtless many authors have explored these various sections of philosophy in turn, but there are a goodly number of those who have specialized in one of the branches exclusively, so this division seems the most convenient.

The metaphysicians must in their turn be divided into idealists and materialists, even though there are those who have passed from one camp into the other, after the example of Li Shih-ts'en, whom we have examined above. The idealists themselves are divided into Kantians, Hegelians, Bergsonians, Platonists, etc. To tell the truth, hardly any follow one system exclusively—all are eclectics; but since in general they manifest some preferences for a particular author, we shall therefore place them among the followers of this master.

Chang Tung-sun, the neo-Kantian socialist

The best representative of Occidental philosophy is incontrovertibly Chang Tung-sun. From as early as the age of eighteen, when he read a classic treatise of Buddhism, he had awakened in him a lively penchant for philosophy. After having finished his studies at Tokyo University, he returned to China to devote himself to university teaching and the editing of various reviews. Observing that Chinese philosophers had searched into the problem of the 'Good', or the moral problem, and neglected the problem of the 'True', or the logical problem, he concluded that this negligence had been one of the major reasons for the lack of science in China; for according to him Occidental science was bound up with the interest taken by the philosophers in the problem of knowledge. From then on he devoted himself to the study of all the authors who have gone deeply into epistemology: Plato, Hume, Kant, William James, Dewey, Russell and Bergson, and he translated certain of the *Dialogues* of Plato and the works of Bergson. From that study he derived an eclectic system dominated especially by the influence of Kant, Lewis, Morgan and Wundt.

His point of departure is then the problem of knowledge. To proceed from psychology like W. James, from biology like Bergson, from physics like Russell, or from ethics like Plato, seemed to him less happy. The object of knowledge is a very complex world. There is a world of infrastructures: that is, a world of phenomena of the natural world, which seems like something plastic, elastic. There is a world of sensation: being intermediate between subject and object, and hence probably illusory and without reality, sensation is at most indicative of the external world. There is a world of structures: although permanent and definite in themselves, the infrastructures seem plastic or elastic according to sensation, in such a way that we can construct images and project them on them. Lastly, there is the world of interpretations: not only do we construct many 'fictions', but we try to make them intelligible; and from this come all sorts of explanations of the world—scientific, philosophic, aesthetic, moral and religious. In consideration of these multiple factors of knowledge, he calls his system 'epistemological pluralism'. In the main he is inspired by the critical philosophy of Kant, but he is at variance with it on some important points. In particular he denies that the order of the external world is a product of the synthesizing power of the mind and that the data of sensation are the material of knowledge. The exterior world is the world of laws.

The consequence of this rejection of sensation is a radical negation of the concept of substance. Since order, or law, constitutes the truth of the external world, that is nothing more than empty structure, without reality, whence the name 'panstructuralism' which he gives to his cosmology. 'I consider', he says, 'that there is neither matter, nor spirit, nor life, but only *structures*. . . . Matter is an empty term which corresponds to nothing existent. The same goes for the concepts of life and spirit. . . . We prefer to substitute the physical laws for matter, the biological laws for life, and the psychological laws for spirit. Thus there are physical laws and not matter, biological laws and not life, psychological laws and not spirit. In other words, all is structure, there is no substance; and these structures cannot be free of our consciousness. Thus it is with the flowers in a mirror: they lose neither their colour nor their form— but they are in the mirror.'[1] In short the concept of substance, an inheritance from Aristotelian thought, does not seem to him more than a term, a convenient hypothesis, which is at bottom only a lazy habit of thought. Mathematical formulas, on the contrary, bring us much closer to matter. 'In reality, that which we know of truth in connection with matter reduces itself to mathematical formulas.'[2] Let us also banish for ever this concept of 'substance' as disastrous to our thinking. 'The terms matter, life, and spirit, are only concepts, which have no more reality than the terms "great" or "beautiful". . . . In short "matter" is the general term which designates the physical laws; if one adds the biological laws to the physical laws, one obtains the concept of "life". Finally, if one joins the psychological laws to the preceding, one gets the concept of "spirit".'[3] In other words, the world is only 'structure'.

From this cosmological system the author draws his conception of life. Although the world is only structure, it evolves without ceasing, giving birth to new species. The discovery of this truth inaugurates a new and very fruitful era in the field of thought. Always it is necessary to establish a distinction between 'becoming' and 'evolution': becoming implies the idea of necessity, whereas evolution is connected with the idea of liberty. This conception of evolution governs our conception of life. The moral judgment which makes us condemn a bad action definitely proves evolution. Civilized man was not made in a day. He has had to pass through many inferior stages in order to arrive at his present stage. In the course of history he has at the same time augmented his scientific knowledge and developed his moral judgment, thanks to individual heredity and social experiences. Man commenced by groping, and little by little he discovered all the principles of ethics. The development of man is then twofold, intellectual and moral; knowledge and conduct are inseparable. Thanks to his reason man is conscious of this development; this possibility of intellectual and moral self-cultivation is the great nobility of man, his superiority over the animal. He can transform his natural, instinctive, animal life into an ideal, rational life, animated by a purpose. In this march to the ideal, our reason runs into the obstacle of the passions, and the policy to hold in regard to them is, from the positive point of view, to 'sublimate' them, and from the negative point of view, to 'curb' them.

On the other hand the individual who works towards the perfection of his moral life necessarily has relations with society. While he influences society, it in turn reacts on him: they correct each other. It is useless to curse civilization: it is necessary to work for its progress and to try to establish an ideal society. Moreover the continuity of society poses the problem of immortality. The immortality of society is evident, but does this apply also to immortality of the soul? In these latter years there have been many experiments on this subject. They have not led to any result, and the question remains in suspense. 'It is a point well worthy of remark: today the great number of scholars are inclined towards an attitude of doubt; they no longer deny categorically as in the past. For me also it is an unresolved question. At the present time, to contend that nothing subsists after death is a premature matter.'[4] An honest admission, quite rare among the modern thinkers of China, among whom belief in materialistic positivism has done away with all metaphysical doubt of this kind. Still, his thought does not rise higher; he does not set up the hypothesis of a God. In this, therefore, he is illogical. Chang Tung-sun believes that even if science were to prove the immortality of the soul by experimental methods, the ideal of man would not be radically changed. Man must by any hypothesis continue to perfect himself and to make civilization progress. The ideal will always be to try to transcend himself. The first step on this path is 'knowledge'; that is the reason why thinkers have all (*sic*) advocated idealism. The second and most important step is moral progress. The whole constitutes 'culture'. 'Morals is integrated into all culture, and the progress of morals follows the progress of culture. The evolution of morals entails the evolution of other co-relative aspects of culture, such as economics, politics, and technology.'[5] The ideal remains always inaccessible. Hence progress has no end, and the development of morals is unlimited.

This emphasis on the evolution of liberty is the reflection of his temperament. A very liberal and changeable spirit, he is himself the appropriate illustration of his theories. During the war his thought underwent a profound evolution. He abandoned metaphysics for sociology, and this involved another philosophy. 'Not long ago I was studying the problem of knowledge especially according to Kant; but since then I have changed, I have studied it from the standpoint of sociology; I have turned to the social studies with much interest and ceased to be a specialist in the mysteries of metaphysics. Thus I have simultaneously studied epistemology and sociology. Very few have noticed this change, for they go by my former books when studying me. Epistemological sociology is a new science, still young; it was Karl Marx who founded it. By it we can begin to study philosophy.'[6] Such were the words with which he addressed the students of Peking University in April 1947. Indeed, during his imprisonment under the Japanese occupation, he had had the leisure to reflect and to write. The result was the publication in 1946 of three works, in which he brings to the fore his reflections concerning the concepts of democracy and society. Long imbued with idealistic and liberal socialism, he had always been opposed to the Kuomintang as well as the Communist Party. Because of this same liberalism, he wanted neither the political hegemony of the first, nor a bloody revolution. He abandoned his old party and his friend Chang Chün-mai to enter the new party of the Democratic League, and he tried several times to be the bridge in negotiations between Nationalists and Communists. He has therefore turned towards Marx, but still without admitting it, as he finds Marx's angle of vision too narrow. Even though 'class' influences individual thought, it is not the only determining element of thought. 'One can have socialist ideas without belonging to the working class,'[7] according to the example of Marx and Engels themselves.

He suddenly discovers the leading role which the intellectuals must play in guiding politics—a role formerly filled to general satisfaction by the *literati*, who were a counterbalance to imperial absolutism. He thus reclaims for them the right and the duty to direct the democratic movement since, as the evolution of the Occident shows, democracy and socialism seem to be the only possible orthodoxy in politics. Entrusting peasants with the guiding of themselves does not make sense. The intellectuals play this role in two ways: either by teaching, or by collaboration with the peasants in the campaign—which presupposes the return of students to the interior, instead of residing in the cities. The agrarian problem preoccupies him. He has been quite a supporter of the 'collective farms', but without demanding the abolition of private property. Further, the acquisition of science must be accompanied by moral education. He complains precisely because this second part of the ideal is forgotten. The attitude of the *literati* of other days is disappearing more and more, save among a few thinkers such as Ma I-fu, Liang Shu-ming or Hsiung Shih-li. He declares that the leftward tendency augments this state of mind, for Marx repudiated the absolute character of morals. On this point he remains faithful to Kant. 'The intellectuals who are appearing in these latter years, after having embraced materialism, strive still less to be gentlemen.'[8] In short, his thought veers towards Marx, but still resists: he does not completely renounce his old ideal.

Since then his thought has further evolved. In 1947 he published a small tract of 95 pages, in which he is seen to be more resolutely committed to the Marxian way. The theme of this little book is that today democracy and socialism are synonymous. If we grant there was a time when Marxism and democracy were hateful, it was because democracy in the nineteenth century had deviated by depending upon capitalism. In reality socialism alone is the democratic orthodoxy. He concludes: 'Not only have we proved that Marxism is democracy, but also we say that the ideal elements constituting Marxism are the same as those of anarchism. Marxism recognizes the State in the countries of today as nothing more than an organism by which the possessing classes administer their common interests. Therefore, on the day when the classes have disappeared, the State will follow into oblivion in their train.'[9] And some lines later he adds, after having shown that the ultimate aim of Marxism is the abolition of the State and even of work: 'As for me, speaking of the ideal, I personally hold to anarchism. Government is an organism which uses authority, and all authority has a constraining character. If one wishes the maximum liberty, he must not be under the domination of anyone.'[10]

The intellectual itinerary of Chang Tung-sun has surprised and scandalized several of his friends, and he has broken with them. It certainly is not common to see an adversary of Marxism end up in the camp of his enemies and adore that which he had branded. It is the result of an uncurbed liberalism which does not rest on any solid principle. In another sense than his, we can apply to him his own theories: absolute evolution leads to anarchy!

If Chang Tung-sun might still be considered a Kantian because of his metaphysics, this being the principal influence to which he refers, there are many other thinkers who merit the same courtesy. Cheng Hsin is considered as being the first to have introduced Kant, whose warmest partisan he is: 'I believe that the philosophy of Kant is the highest good sense in philosophy.'[11] Mou Tsung-san has stressed the Kantian critique of reason, and he has tried to interpret the *I Ching* and its diagrams with the principles of Whitehead. He has explored the spirit of Chinese philosophy in order to show that the practical reason of Kant surpasses the theoretical reason.

Various idealisms: Hegelian, Platonic, etc.

Although Kantism thus exercised a certain influence in China, that of Hegel was certainly more important. We have already mentioned Ho Lin as being a specialist on Hegel. He is not alone. Chang Chen-ju, who studied more than ten years in America, England and Germany, having written his thesis at Oxford on *The Moral Philosophy of Hegel*, returned to China to take a chair of philosophy at Peking University, where he taught the philosophy of Kant and Hegel. Shih Yu-chung published in 1943 an introduction to metaphysics under the title *Mind* (説 心); but the critics affirm that it is above all an introduction to the metaphysics of Hegel. For the rest the Anglo-Saxon neo-Hegelianism of Bradley and Bosanquet has furnished him with many of his elements. Here are some of his formulas: 'The mind is the substance, the *noumenon*, experience is the *phenomenon*.' According to him all logical principle, all moral and aesthetic law, all religious dogma, is innate in the heart and develops by contact with matter; consequently the mind governs reality and the latter serves as its instrument. 'It is aesthetic experience which is the meeting place between spirit and matter. . . . Each forgets itself: the subject and the object are made one.'[12] In short, to judge from the bent of his thought, he is a subjective idealist.

For his part Hsieh Yu-wei has instead followed Anglo-Saxon neo-realism, which is itself under the influence of the neo-Hegelianism of Bradley and Royce. He has not published a personal system, but has devoted himself to critical essays on contemporary thinkers. In the most recent of his works, *Critique of the Masterpieces of Contemporary Philosophy* (現 代 哲 學 名 著 述 評) (1947), he analyses the following authors: Hsiung Shih-li, Ho Lin and Chang Shih-chao, for China; Dewey, Price, Hume, Adler, Whitehead, Croce, Alexander and Tagore, among the foreigners. He also discusses at length the principal respective characteristics of the philosophies of China and the Occident. His conclusion is that ancient Chinese philosophy is idealistic, with a practical spirit, utilizing the method of intuition and showing a religious attitude, whereas modern Chinese philosophy, which still inclines towards idealism, considers theory and practice of the same importance, completes intuition by reason and adopts a philosophical attitude. Modern Occidental thought seems to him to be summed up in six points: (1) the identity of Heaven and Man, or a revolt against dualism, (2) a revolt against matter, (3) a tendency towards idealism, as a corollary to (2), (4) preponderance accorded to the idea of value, (5) attention paid to history, to the times, (6) and finally minute exactitude of analysis by following scientific methods and mathematical logic. In short, Hsieh Yu-wei is a convinced idealist.

Still in the line of idealism but closer to spiritualism than all the others, is Fu T'ung-hsien, professor of philosophy in St. John's University, Shanghai. In 1933 he published his first book, *The Problem of Knowledge* (知 識 論 綱). In the preface he announces that his studies of the past two or three years have been concentrated on this problem, and that he has read successively the works of Locke, Berkeley, Kant, Hegel and Feuerbach. His book is merely a critical analysis of the principal theories of knowledge. He concludes by aligning himself in the camp of objective idealism. In practice he ends up in conceptualism, like so many of his predecessors.

His latest works, *Philosophy and Life* (哲 學 與 人 生) (1947), and *Outline of Aesthetics* (美 學 綱 要) (1948), develop idealistic thought in ethics and in aesthetics. In the first he begins by mentioning the rather general tendency to laxity of morals, due to the troubled circumstances of China. That is why he wants to set forth the elements of the conduct of life, the section of philosophy which he thinks the most important. He establishes the essential characteristics of human nature, the sources of moral judgment, the social influences which modify it, the elements of the conscience which pass judgment on good and evil, the effect of the family and the school on the formation of the heart; and he believes that moral judgment progresses with the complexity of life and the acquisition of knowledge. He also analyses at length the influence of religion on morals. He affirms that far from it being 'the opium of the people', religion drives man to correct himself and to improve society. Thus it is one of the most powerful forces at the service of humanity. 'The religious experience is a complex psychological state made up of the union of many aspects: the pure sentiment of love, the supreme ideal good of morals, the aesthetic sense of literary art, the wisdom of the mind . . . by which one can reach the ideal world of pure love, pure beauty, pure truth, and pure goodness. But this complex, transcendent, ideal world cannot be attained by the majority of men.'[13] The author also surveys the various religions which have a universal character: Buddhism, Christianity, and Mohammedanism. However, despite all the esteem which he attaches to religions, he does not seem personally to adhere to any. He finds that it is best not to flee from reality, but to strive to realize happiness on earth, to struggle to bring about the ideal of a world perfectly true, good, and beautiful. Yesterday man struggled against nature, today he fights against society, tomorrow he will battle against himself. In short, in this march towards the ideal, man follows human reason.

Among these three values of truth, goodness, and beauty, he

appears to award the palm to the last. In his latest work he says: 'Art, one can say, is the soul of human life. If mankind did not have art, it would lead a cold and mechanical life like the animals. Art is the manifestation of human progress.'[14]

T'ang Chün-i, another Hegelian, should be mentioned. Resolutely emphasizing the primacy of spirit, he is interested above all in the moral problem. For this reason we shall study him later.

Aside from Hegelian idealism and Bergsonian idealism, the two principal Occidental idealistic currents in China, there is still a place for others. If the ancient philosophy of Greece merits a mention again in the history of modern philosophy in China, it is assuredly thanks to the work of Ch'en K'ang, specialist in Plato, and the first Chinese to approach this philosophy directly by the Greek text. After ten years of study in Germany, he set himself to prove that Aristotle was not at all the adversary of Plato, but, contrary to general opinion, his continuator. It is in this sense that he has translated the *Parmenides* and annotated it according to the classical method. His very personal commentary is almost ten times as long as the text itself. Since before the war, from 1934, he has attracted attention in philosophical circles by his various studies of the problem of knowledge according to Plato. While still in Germany he wrote a book on *The Problem of Distinction in the Philosophy of Aristotle* (亞里士多德哲學中之分離問題) which was probably his thesis for the doctorate.

The Marxists: Li Ta, Ai Ssu-ch'i

The posterity of Hegel was not only idealism. A whole school took his method while taking the opposite to his spirit, namely dialectical materialism. On the part of the Marxists this relationship is so conscious that, shortly after 1931, for the centenary of the celebrated philosopher, it was a Marxist, Yeh Ch'ing, who took the initiative in commemorating this anniversary by publishing a collection of studies entitled *Hegel* (黑格爾), with an appendix on Feuerbach. Logically then, after the representatives of the Hegelian right, it is necessary to point out the leftists who claim Hegel as teacher.

We have already presented the two earliest theoreticians of Marxism in China, Ch'en Tu-hsiu and Li Ta-chao; but, as we saw, their writings were only fragmentary. The first to be a systematic interpreter of Marx was Li Ta. After having several times gone to Japan to study economics, he finally returned to China in 1918, and almost at once entered the Communist party. As a university professor after 1923, he taught economics, law and sociology. Meanwhile he published some treatises on economics and on Marxist philosophy and translated the classical commentaries of Marx, Engels and Lenin. In philosophy his principal work is a weighty tome of more than 800 pages, whose fourth edition came out in 1939. It is a complete account of Marxist sociology, or the materialist conception of history, and of dialectical materialism. The title, *Elements of Sociology* (社會學大綱), gives a poor indication of the contents. It is a veritable compendium of Marxism, explaining nearly all the important problems raised by Marx and his disciples. It is according to our knowledge the most learned work published in China on this school. In concluding the author comments thus upon the Marxist formula, 'religion, opium of the people': 'The Church preaches peace between classes in order to get the workers to oppose socialism and support the vexations of capitalism. . . . In order to carry out this task, the Church has created numerous workers' organizations which are united with the bourgeois political institutions. . . . Besides this very important reactionary task which it performs within, the Church also plays the role of harbinger of imperialistic aggressions in colonial territory. . . . In the colonized territories the missionaries outwardly undertake the preaching of Christianity, but in reality they practice espionage or commerce. On this point China is an excellent example.'[15] Evidently this well-known line of reasoning does not presuppose the least reliance on facts. Faith in the words of the Master is so strong that a man believes it possible to dispense with exact verification of his assertions—an attitude which is neither realistic nor scientific. Marx cannot be deluded; if he put forth naïve ideas, it is better to remain blind than to cast any doubt on the least of his dogmas!

Thus religion, alleged to be responsible for all crimes, will not be able to subsist in the city of the future. The author concludes with this prophetic vision of the future: 'The extinction of religion will not be a peaceable era; it will be an era of violent struggles. When socialism shall prosper, religion will entirely disappear. But, in the preceding stage called the period of "reform", it keeps its reactionary role. The enemies of socialism always use religion as a weapon and seek all sorts of expedients to prevent its extinction. . . . The militant materialists, having brought to light the deep-seated reasons for the survival of religion in the womb of capitalism, believe that in order to combat religion it is necessary not to be content with an abstract ideology. It is necessary that this ideological struggle be united with concrete action aimed at extirpating the social roots of religion. And so religion will be extinguished little by little in the course of this stage.'[16] With this penetrating verdict he finishes the eight hundred and fifty-fourth, the last page of the volume!

More recently Li Ta has republished the second part of the same work on historical materialism under the title *Modern Sociology* (現 代 社 會 學) (1947), without any appreciable changes. This book was not long for sale in the booksellers' windows, as the Kuomintang censor promptly proscribed it. Clients were notified to look for it in Hong Kong. But the advertisement announces that in a collection entitled 'University', the author has prepared new treatises on the same subject. It is needless to add that one should not look for the least originality of thought in these works.

The rival of the preceding, both in seniority and in learned manner, is Li Chi. After having finished his studies in Germany, he returned just in time to begin to publish his studies on Marxism in *La Jeunesse* alongside Ch'en Tu-hsiu, Li Ta-chao and Li Ta. Afterwards he took part in the first Marxist argument on conceptions of Chinese history and prepared a general critique on it. Likewise he criticized the *History of Chinese Philosophy* of Hu Shih, from the Marxist point of view. But his principal claim to glory rests on his monumental *Biography of Marx* (馬 克 思 傳) in three volumes (still being republished), in which he recounts the life of his hero and describes at length the genesis and contents of his writings. Basically the book is an exposition of Marxist doctrines placed in their historical framework—a less arid form than that of the systematic treatises. Despite his merits, Li Chi has been little talked about, since he was for long suspect in the eyes of the orthodox Marxists because of his Trotskyist tendencies. In fact he was expelled from the Communist party along with Ch'en Tu-hsiu and followed his leader into the opposition party which formed immediately after his expulsion. He even received in it the title of 'Commissar of Agriculture'. This was obviously a purely honorary title, since this 'Trotskyist' party was ephemeral, but it reveals to us another activity of Li Chi, that of specialist in the study of agriculture according to the socialist methods. He has translated a work on this subject, and the advertisement tells us that the translator has had forty years of experience in this field. His intimacy with Ch'en Tu-hsiu has greatly damaged his reputation, and he does not seem to have been pardoned as yet. If the very recent republication of his *Biography of Marx* would lead us to suppose a return to grace, it must be noted on the other hand that his name does not figure on the list of members of the Cultural Committee recently appointed by the 'People's Government'.

On the other hand a philosopher assuredly in favour at court is Ai Ssu-ch'i, who may almost be considered as the official thinker of the party, in view of his positions of service and the success of his books. He appeared for the first time in intellectual circles about the year 1934 and has been conspicuous since the beginning by his virulent attacks against Yeh Ch'ing, his less orthodox rival. At first he edited in Shanghai a Marxist review called *Intellectual Life* (讀書生活), published by a society of the same name. When the war against Japan broke out in 1937, he became a refugee in Yenan, the capital of the Soviet State of Shensi, and was there president of a philosophical society. Among his works the most celebrated is unquestionably his *Philosophy of the People* (大眾哲學), first published in 1936[17] under the title *Talks on Philosophy* (哲學講話). A masterpiece of popularization, with an unheard-of success: thirty-two editions in twelve years! The new editions have been liberally revised and enlarged, for the author no longer has to fear censorship; but curiously enough they seem less attractive. This is because a certain vagueness was more advantageous than a too blunt explanation. The success of this work, indicative of the favour met with by new ideas, is due especially to its excellent presentation of the doctrine. The author succinctly describes in it the essential points of the Marxist dialectic, while illustrating them with numerous examples borrowed from the happenings of the day, from screen celebrities, or from national stories; while the dryness of the account is always tempered by concrete, picturesque, even humorous reflections, which makes reading it considerably easier for the reader. Above all this is a work of propaganda, not a learned work in the style of the two preceding Marxists, Li Ta and Li Chi. The aim is to infuse into the people the principles of dialectical materialism, so as to give them the guiding compass for thought, behaviour and action. 'Each man has his own ideas which come from his heredity, from the milieu, and from various circumstances—ideas which are not always sound and exact. It is important to rectify them. This is the mission of progressive philosophy. It helps us to penetrate problems more quickly and more exactly, to destroy all mystery, to discover the origin of all things, to combat all oppression.'[18] Our spontaneous ideas, under the sway of fatalism, despair, or some other cause, often drive us to suicide or to a pessimism which negates all effort. To remedy these disastrous psychological deviations, in view of the small number of specialists in philosophy, 'we are forced to seek to know the authentic philosophy. The essential role of philosophy is indeed to give us the solutions to problems of life; it should guide us in practice, for its final task is the reform of the world'.[19] Then the author sets himself to find among all the systems of thought the one which deserves the title of 'the authentic philosophy'. He ends by concluding that only dialectical materialism answers all the needs of man, being the summit of human thought and the last word of science, since it possesses the scientific method *par excellence*, namely the materialistic dialectic! Such is the way the problem of Marxism is stated in most of these little popularizing manuals.

Aside from this slender little book, the author has also written a series of propaganda brochures, such as *How to Study Philosophy* (知何研究哲學), and *On How to Think* (思想方法) (1935), as well as collections of various essays, simple answers to the difficulties of the reader, such as *Philosophy and Life* (哲學與生活) (1937), and *Practice and Theory* (實踐與理論) (1939).

Many other names are also known among the Marxist writers, such as Shen Chih-yüan, Ch'en Wei-shih, and Huang T'e. Shen Chih-yüan, a former student in Japan, is also a specialist in popularization. His works diverge in two directions, economics and philosophy, and he has translated various classical treatises of Marx and his commentators. Most especially, Shen Chih-yüan has been editor of the review, *Theory and Reality* (理 論 與 現 實), which brought together on its editorial staff the great names of the Marxist intelligentsia in all the branches of culture; philosophy, economics, history, literature, and science. It was the best journal of ideas published in China along this line. Begun at the end of 1939, it was still in existence after the victory over Japan in 1946; but then it disappeared, doubtless by order of the Nationalist censor. Its editor has since been named as a member of the Committee of Education and Culture of the 'People's Government'.

Ch'en Wei-shih has written several works on dialectical materialism, of which the most important is *Talks on the System of the New Philosophy* (新 哲 學 體 系 講 話) published in 1937. This stout volume of 400 pages, one of the most highly developed of the type, has as its main characteristic the refutation of adverse systems, while building up little by little the outline of Marxism. However, Chen's books dating from before the war have not been republished, and his name itself has not reappeared. Perhaps the man is deceased.

Huang T'e is a new author who appeared suddenly in Shanghai during the Sino-Japanese War, publishing three or four Marxist brochures one after the other. But his name relapsed almost immediately into oblivion (was it not perhaps a camouflage, a pseudonym?). He fought against Yeh Ch'ing, the turncoat of Marxism, and in favour of 'The New Democracy' of Mao Tse-tung. Hu Sheng is a popularizer, the author of slim volumes of fifty or sixty pages in which the essentials of Marxism are well stated. During the Sino-Japanese War he collaborated in Chungking in editing *Theory and Reality*, and himself published another Marxist doctrinal review.

A small group of intellectuals have specialized in the history of Marxist philosophy. Besides Kuo Mo-jo, of whom we have already spoken, we must mention here Ch'en Po-ta, Hsiang Lin-ping, and Hou Wai-lu. Ch'en Po-ta, a specialist in critical studies on antiquity and modern times, has not to our knowledge written any complete works explaining dialectical materialism. During the war he was in Yenan, collaborating with Ai Ssu-ch'i and his Marxist-educated group. He developed the philosophical aspect of the slogan put out by Mao Tse-tung on January 1, 1940, in favour of a 'New Democracy'. Hsiang Lin-ping, who belonged to the editorial committee of *Theory and Reality*, is hardly known except by his critical studies on ancient and modern Chinese philosophy. His principal work is an *Outline of the History of Chinese Philosophy* (中 國 哲 學 史 綱要) (1939), surveyed from the angle of dialectical materialism. Hou Wai-lu was also an editor of the review, *Theory and Reality*. In 1942 he brought out a *History of Thought and Scholarship in Ancient China* (中 國 古 代 思 想 學 術 史), in which he examines all the problems pending in intellectual circles relating to high antiquity—this of course in the light of Marxist principles—and concludes that the wisdom of ancient China surpassed the Hellenic culture. In 1947 he published two voluminous tomes on the *History of Thought and Scholarship in Modern China* (近 代 中 國 思 想 學 術 史), in which he shows that since the seventeenth century it has not been inferior to that of the Renaissance in Europe.

One could add many other names, nearly all of them translators or popularizers. The dominant preoccupation is not so much to go deeply into, as to spread, the dialectical method and the principles of materialism. The authors do not seek to write personal, original works. They use and abuse repetition. For them Marxism is above all a doctrine of life, of action; and so speculation in itself does not interest them. Therefore they neglect profound studies. Some Marxists themselves have complained: 'The various works on new philosophy [i.e. Marxism] published this year are for the most part collections of essays or works of popularization. Truly it must be said that deep, original works of philosophy are rare. The philosophical level of the readers is extremely low. Besides, the manuals of popular philosophy abound with errors and superficial passages.'[20] The Congress of Marxist Philosophy held in Russia in 1947 made the same complaints.

The scientific materialist: Yeh Ch'ing

On the borderline of the Marxist group one must take note of Yeh Ch'ing, whose works have caused much spilling of ink between 1935 and 1937, and who was moreover at the beginning one of the leaders of Marxist thought. After having studied in France, he returned at first to his natal province of Szechuan, and then came to Shanghai to establish and manage a book-store with the significant name, 'The Thinking Bookshop' (辛 狠 書 店).[21] While this book-shop had as yet been going only a few years it did considerable work in the field of philosophical publications. It published at first the French materialists of the eighteenth century, la Mettrie, d'Holbach, Helvetius, Condillac and Diderot; and then those of ancient Greece, Heraclitus, Democritus and Epicurus; certain more or less orthodox Marxists, like Plekhanov, Déborin, Bogdanov and Lafargue; finally, the great scientific synthesists, Planck, Jeans, Eddington, Huxley, Pearson and Einstein. A mere enumeration is eloquent enough by itself: it tells us already of the general tendencies of the publisher.

In the review *Twentieth Century* (二 十 世 紀), Yeh Ch'ing undertakes a general criticism of the great masters of contemporary Chinese thought. As it happens, he did not carry through his plan, for he stopped after having prepared a very detailed, critical analysis of only two authors, Hu Shih and Chang Tung-sun. Because of these critiques he was hailed as one of the new leaders of Marxist thought. His studies had as their goal to prepare him in the working out of a system. This he reached much more quickly than he had foreseen, and, abandoning his initial plan, he began to publish the fruits of his reflections. Such was the origin of his first speculative essay, *Whither Philosophy?* (哲 學 到 何 處 去) (1934). Taking up anew the thesis of two obscure Russian philosophers, Minin and Enchumen, he announced the forthcoming extinction of philosophy, by virtue of the law of universal evolution which requires that all that is born grows and dies. Formerly philosophy, by disclaiming religion, brought about its disappearance. Likewise science, from the fact that it has broken with philosophy to live independently, must logically bring about its decline. The pure Marxists accuse Yeh Ch'ing of the false interpretation of certain texts of Engels, and of reviving the error of the Russian mechanists. They admit the future disappearance of non-Marxist philosophy, but energetically maintain that Marxism will not perish, since it is the scientific method *par excellence*.

Yeh Ch'ing however repeated his offence. In *Problems of Philosophy*

(哲 學 問 題) (1936), he takes up the same doctrine again from another slant. Idealism and materialism, he says, each contain a part of the truth: they must be amalgamated in order to complement each other. Thus a place is left for materialism. Did not Marx himself give the example by affecting the synthesis of Hegelian idealism with the materialism of Feuerbach? In consequence of this higher synthesis the eternal conflict between idealism and materialism has vanished. 'Since the oppositions are resolved, and opposition was the motivating force of its development, the history of philosophy stops. Is this the end of philosophy? Obviously. That is a natural and inevitable conclusion.'[22] The system which results from this definitive synthesis has changed its nature and is now only the 'science of thought'.

At bottom the debate resolves itself into a question of words. Yeh Ch'ing wants to call philosophy the 'science of thought'. His adversaries retort that to identify Marxism with science is to narrow it by depriving it of its social basis and historical meaning, because historical and social problems are an indispensable source of the development of dialectical materialism. In short, instead of exalting its importance, Yeh Ch'ing ends in fact by ruining it, by undermining its bases. Marxism claims certainly to rest on Darwinism, but by going beyond it, adds to it living, historical, social experience. Yeh Ch'ing is also accused of following 'the line of Bernstein, Kautsky, Bogdanov, Trotsky and Bukharin', that is to say, of all the heretical interpreters of Marxist thought.

The discussions between the two camps were not confined to this question. Many others which were very important were debated, such as the problem of the relations between formal logic and dialectic, the problem of internal and external cause, and the problem of theory and practice. Moreover these arguments reflected the battle of ideas which had gripped the Soviet intellectuals ten years earlier. Yeh Ch'ing defended himself with a dialectical vigour and a prolificness of writing which his adversaries had to envy. He himself brought together the essays of the two opposing parties in two volumes under the title of *The Controversies of the New Philosophy* (新 哲 學 論 戰 集) (1936), and *Struggles in the Developing of the New Philosophy* (為 發 展 新 哲 學 而 戰) (1937). The breaking out of the Sino-Japanese War put a stop to the discussions, but the animosity between the two camps did not cease for the duration. In 1940, attacks against Yeh Ch'ing were again to be found in the Marxist reviews, and he on his part, crowning all his disputes, declared petulantly in 1939: 'Marx was not the inventor of dialectic. Moreover dialectic and proletariat are not related, and dialectic and socialism are not related, hence dialectical materialism and communism are not related.'[23]

The root of the trouble is that the Marxism of Yeh Ch'ing is too eclectic, too original, too remote from the usual path. For him Marx is neither god nor prophet, but one philosopher among others, who did not necessarily say the last word on all problems. Although a convinced materialist, Yeh Ch'ing refuses to be servile to one thinker to the prejudice of others: he keeps his independence.

Not long ago there gravitated around him a whole group of philosophers and translators—Yang Po-k'ai, Jen Pei-kuo, Wang T'e-fu, and T'an Fu-chih—of whom several have since attacked him and rejoined the ranks of orthodox Marxism. Others remain under his influence, namely Yang Po-k'ai and Wang T'e-fu. Yang Po-k'ai translated the Greek materialists (Epicurus and Heraclitus) and the French materialists (d'Holbach, Diderot, Helvetius and Condillac), and devoted himself to criticism of various theoreticians, in the review *Twentieth Century* (二 十 世 紀) of which he was the editor. To show the general spirit of this review, the mouthpiece of the group, it is sufficient to quote the plan of the authors in the advertising prospectus: 'The present review treats of theoretical science, is devoted to criticism of thought, and to ideological construction. It seeks to judge history and theory by relying upon scientific truth. Its task is the unification of science and philosophy, of creating a theoretical system of natural sciences, of blending the social sciences and the natural sciences, and of constructing the science of thought.' Ambitious projects, they are exactly word for word the ideal towards which, as we have seen, all the efforts of Yeh Ch'ing converge.

The other author who has worked in the same direction and has shown a certain constructive spirit in the manner of Yeh Ch'ing, is Wang T'e-fu. He, unlike the Marxists, no longer sought to popularize, but instead to deepen, in the same way as the two foregoing. The enumeration of his publications is enough to show this. In the space of a few years he wrote a whole series of works studying matter, as follows: *What Is Matter?* (甚麼叫物質), *Treatise on Physics* (物理學概論), *The Formation of the World* (世界生成論), and *System of Anthropology* (人類學體系).[24] Thus it is really the philosophy of nature which the author aspires to construct. One cannot say, however, that he has been very original or profound as Yeh Ch'ing has.

Another thinker of the same group, Chang I-hung, published his *Elements of Philosophy* (哲學概論) in 1936. This teaches the 'scientism' so much in favour today. It concludes with these words: 'Science is, one can say, the highest restoration of religion, but in it reason is substituted for faith, proof for imagination, and man, the slave of nature, has thereby become its master.' This is the religion of science!

In sum this materialist movement which is dissident from Marxism is none other than the old scientific positivism—quite out-moded today—joined to a socialism which is rather vaguely tinged with Marxism. The movement was very active during the years which immediately preceded the Sino-Japanese War; and even though it has by now completely disappeared as a group phenomenon, the ideas expressed by its adepts constitute a credo which has spread very widely in the world of contemporary Chinese thought.

This rapid excursion into the idealistic and materialistic systems of modern China has not yet allowed us to pass in review all the thinkers of some importance. Having named the representatives of general philosophy, it now remains for us to glance at those who are specialists in one or another of the divisions of philosophy, namely logic, ethics, and aesthetics.

The specialists in logic: Chin Yüeh-lin

Throughout the course of its history Chinese thought has given all its attention to the moral problem, and neglected the study of nature; it has been almost exclusively anthropocentric. 'The supreme goal of philosophy in the eyes of the Chinese philosopher, was to develop his own personality and that of others, and to progress towards wisdom. . . . Consequently, it has adopted as its method intuition, or dogmatism. Lacking the speculative spirit and logical experimentation, it has proceeded by categorical affirmation without seeking for proof.'[25] These words are by Hsieh Yu-wei. For his part Fung Yu-lan has remarked that if China has not speculated on the outside world with a natural intellectual curiosity, if it has not created science, it is 'because of all philosophies the Chinese philosophy is the most human and the most practical. . . . The West is extension, the East is intension; . . . the West emphasizes what we have, the East emphasizes what we are.'[26] In consequence the modern thinkers have put all their efforts into supplying the missing logical method.

Since the first years of the twentieth century, thinkers and translators have endeavoured to introduce Occidental logic. Yen Fu translated the *Logic* of John Stuart Mill in 1902, and then the *Logic* of E. Jenks in 1905. Ch'en Ta-ch'i, who had studied in Japan and Germany, returned to teach in Peking University, and specialized in the study of this science. He wrote a number of articles and even a treatise, *Elements of Logic* (論理學概論).[27] Next there was Hu Shih, whose whole intellectual effort is summed up in the propagation and application of the pragmatic method of thought, which he considers as the type *par excellence* of the scientific method. At about the same time the Russellian or mathematical method recruited many supporters. These two types of logic, the pragmatic and the mathematical, flourished especially around 1920 to 1923, but continue still to hold a far from negligible place in intellectual circles. After that date, towards 1927, there was a growing infatuation with the Marxist logic, or dialectical materialism: 'If the experimental logic of Dewey and the mathematical logic of Russell have had their day,' says an historian of modern thought in China, 'now they have lost their authority. They have been supplanted by a new philosophical method, the Dialectic.'[28] Moreover, the champions of this methodology are not necessarily all Communists; in the domain of thought Marxism and Communism are not exactly identical, and many intellectuals who are devoted to the Marxist method are not bound at the same time to the Communist Party. We are speaking only of fact, not of right. We are not trying to find out whether one can be Marxist without being Communist, logically speaking. Besides, the Marxist dialectic is not an invention of Marx, but is borrowed from Hegel; and, as we have seen, the Hegelian method does not lack partisans. One must then conclude that on the whole, dialectic, be it idealistic (or Hegelian), or be it materialistic (or Marxist), is by far the most widespread method of thought in China.

However, this is not to say that there has not been any Oriental logic. We have seen that Fung Yu-lan has applied himself to reviving a philosophical method inspired in large part by the neo-Confucianism of Chu Hsi, supplemented, it is true, by certain Occidental systems such as the neo-realist American school and the Viennese school. Likewise we have recalled the limited restoration to favour of Hindu or Buddhist logic. Their partisans, however, despite the great name of Fung Yu-lan, constitute only a small minority.

All these efforts to endow China with the ideal method of thought hardly show anything but a docile imitation, and not yet any original construction. However, some thinkers have attempted the latter. The most important is Chin Yüeh-lin. After having finished his studies at Tsinghua University, Peking, he went to America for six years to study political thought, especially that of Green. He then went to Europe for four years. Returning to China in 1926, he taught the history of European political theory at Tsinghua University. Green was not only a theoretician of political science, he was also a philosopher, and his ideas gave his disciple a fondness for philosophy. Chin Yüeh-lin set himself to study systems of logic and various schools of contemporary philosophy, and thus worked out his own, which he gave to the public in a book entitled *Logic* (邏　輯) (1935). He demonstrated a true power of analysis. Some have even gone so far as to reproach him for his extreme closeness of reasoning, strictness, profundity of thought, and a use of symbolical terms and mathematical formulas so excessive as to discourage the non-specialist reader. A critic, in order to explain humorously the somewhat grim aspect of his *Logic*, its pages littered with mathematical formulas, says that Russell himself will be taken aback when he thumbs through it. More recently, in 1940, under the title, *The Tao* (論　道) ('The Way', 'The Doctrine') he made out a whole system of metaphysics, which he based upon three concepts of classical Chinese philosophy—although his terminology differs from that of Fung Yu-lan, the two systems are in reality very much akin in content. Taking expressions borrowed from neo-Confucianism, Chin develops a philosophy inspired by Hume and by Anglo-Saxon neo-realism. This, in the words of the critics, was 'old wine in a new bottle'. Nonetheless, Chin Yüeh-lin remains one of the most distinguished metaphysicians of modern China, endowed with a true creative talent.

Finally, and more recently still, another work attracted the attention of philosophical circles: the *Essentials of Logic* (邏 輯 指 要) (1943) of Professor Chang Shih-chao. Soon after completion of his studies of law in Japan and England he became well-known because of his participation in the Tuan Ch'i-jui government of 1917. At that time he was widely attacked. In this book which he has devoted to logic, he develops and proves with many citations the thesis that the elements of logic are not lacking in the ancient thought of China, but that there has not yet been found the man to join them together into an organic system. He himself does not seem to be the man for this task, since he does not attempt in the slightest a constructive essay to join together these elements.

The philosophy of life of scientific determinism

In short, despite all efforts, logic has not yet driven its roots very deeply into the soil of China, save in the case of Chin Yüeh-lin. One cannot say the same about ethics. We have seen superabundantly that this was the centre of the ancient philosophy, being identified most often with Confucianism. After the furious attacks of which it was the victim between 1915 and 1920, many people felt that this was most regrettable, believing that the new China disowned the old even in that which was most precious. This uneasiness was translated into the debate of 1922 on the philosophies of Orient and Occident, and again into the 1923 controversy of 'science *v.* the philosophy of life', in which the idealists rose against the exaggerated pretensions of science to rule human life. Since under the influence of the Occident many authors did not like to employ the words 'morals', or 'ethics', which seemed reactionary and old fashioned, they preferred to say 'philosophy of life', or 'conception of life', which seemed more modern, more scientific. In truth the two terms are not completely identical, for the philosophy of life overlaps ethics in treating of problems which are not always connected with it. However, the practical difference is not very great, and one can overlook it.

In this new spirit many thinkers have attempted syntheses. The first by date is Shu Hsin-ch'eng, manager of a book-store and author of numerous works on psychology and pedagogy. In 1923, the same year as the celebrated controversy, and obviously in connection with it, he published a *Philosophy of Life* (人 生 哲 學) based upon science, treating of the origin and nature of life, of the place of man in the universe, and of his physical, sentimental, intellectual, social and moral nature. He discusses the problem of the connection of ethics, religion and art with life, but ends by concluding that religion is no longer necessary to human progress. In 1925 Fung Yu-lan also published a *Philosophy of Life* (人 生 哲 學), an adaptation in Chinese of his doctoral dissertation at Columbia University. This was only a synthesis of various schools of Oriental and Occidental thought, romantic (Taoist), idealistic (Plato), nihilistic (Schopenhauer), hedonistic (Yang Chu), utilitarian (Mo Ti), progressivistic (Descartes, Bacon, Fichte), Confucian, Aristotelian, neo-Confucian, Hegelian and neo-realistic. In 1928 Li Shih-ts'en published the first volume of a work bearing the same title and adopting much the same manner of reasoning as Fung Yu-lan. He begins by a critical exposition of Oriental and Occidental theories on the question, and concludes with these words: 'The construction of this science is one of the common goals of humanity. In China it is necessary to put forth a more vigorous effort in this sense, because the philosophy of life of the Orientals surpasses by far that of the Occidentals.'[29] In a word, he proposed Confucianism as the ideal. Again, in 1929, Tu Ya-ch'üan also published a *Philosophy of Life* (人 生 哲 學), in which he built up a system of morals based on the three sciences of biology, psychology, and sociology. He was thus in support of the scientists. However, he borrowed from the streams of thought, ancient and modern, Oriental and Occidental, whatever he thought the best. In particular he carefully studied the various forms of socialism and the economic theories. A short while later he wrote another book on the same subject, *Philosophy of Being in the World* (處 世 哲 學). However, the major portion of Tu's interest is centred upon biology.

To summarize, this new section of philosophy expressed by these four works is an attempt to make morals follow in the wake of science, a course entirely in line with the controversy of 1923 on 'science *v.* the philosophy of life'. The very term 'conception, or philosophy of life' has become very fashionable, and it has gone so far that entire collections of 'conceptions of life' have been published, wherein were inserted the reflections of well-known people. One of these inquiries collected some fifty names, another as many as 250. Even though all tendencies were met with in them, on the whole the positivist point of view prevailed.

The Marxists for their part did not neglect to express their opinion in small, popularized brochures addressed to youth. Thus, Shen Chih-yüan, in *Talks on a New Conception of Life* (新 人 生 觀 講 話) (1936), Hu Sheng, in *The Conception of Life of the New Philosophy* (新 哲 學 的 人 生 觀) (1937), and Ai Ssu-ch'i, in *Philosophy and Life* (哲 學 與 生 活) (1937), take it upon themselves to refute the attacks of the idealists against the lack of morals of the Marxists, and to develop an ethical ideal composed of realism, of combative and scientific revolutionary spirit, of devotion to society, etc. They scoff as much at the 'scientists' as at the 'metaphysicians'. Kautsky's *Ethics and the Materialistic Conception of History* had already been translated three times before 1934.

Semi-Oriental, semi-Occidental rationalistic ethics

Idealism nevertheless produced some works of value with which to oppose the positivistic and Marxist current. Previously we have spoken of the ideas contained in the *Moral Philosophy* (1930) of Chang Tung-sun, a work containing no less than 650 pages. Proceeding in the manner of his predecessors, the author examines successively all the ethical systems since Greek antiquity, but completely neglects Chinese thought. We pass in review successively Socrates, Epicurus, Hobbes, Bentham, Mill, Sidgwick, Clark, Price, Shaftesbury, Hutcheson, Moore, Martineau, Plato, Schopenhauer, von Hartman, Kant, Hume, Adam Smith, Spencer, Darwin, Kropotkin, Guyau, Stephen, Aristotle, Hegel, Bradley and Green.

After this imposing procession, the author dwells upon Wundt and Spranger, with whose opinions he is in close accord. 'My ideal is similar to that of Wundt: it is by culture that I explain ethics.'[30] For him virtue is a value which transcends all the other cultural values—economics, science, politics, art, religion—while at the same time remaining an element of culture, an element which works in concert with the others in the surpassing of the 'self'. In the appendix the author attacks the Marxist ethic and its materialistic conception of history.

In 1935 a certain Huang Fang-kang published an *Ethics* (道德學), which was decidedly Kantian. He established that the methods and principles of ethics have the character of universal laws, just as much as the methods and principles of mathematics and philosophy. 'I boldly declare', he says, 'that the method of ethics is totally *a priori* and transcends experience.'[31] A little farther on he adds: 'All principles, all criteria, which go beyond time and space, which are universal and necessary, cannot be a product of experience; and ethics falls precisely into this category.'[32] This *a priori* moral law is inscribed on the inner hearts of men. Along the same line Huang Fang-kang published a *Socrates* (1935), which also rests upon the Kantian principles.

In 1944 a university professor named Huang Chien-chung published in Chungking a *Comparative Ethics* (比較倫理學), which was widely read. Like the foregoing, he examines the ethical doctrines of both Orient and Occident. The general argument is well described in these words in the preface: 'This book looks for the origin of moral conduct in biology, the origin of moral conscience in sociology, the development of moral ideals in the history of civilizations. Comparison between Orient and Occident shows their resemblances and their differences, their excellences and their deficiencies; the opposition between good and evil gives us the idea of absolute good, and we learn that under the ancient name of 'great harmony' is hidden the new meaning of 'sudden creation'.[33] According to the author the difference between the Orient and the Occident is manifested in five principal points. The Orient has fused morals and politics, has insisted upon the equality of moral duty, is based on the family in order to build up an agricultural state, goes deeply into private, interior morals, and has set up rules of etiquette to preserve order. The Occident, on the contrary, has joined morals with religion, has given all its attention to equality of law, has based an industrial and commercial state upon the individual, has developed a public, exterior ethics, and finally, has made affection or love the basis of family relations. But the differences are small; what is striking is the agreement of views in the majority of cases. From this the author evolves his notion of moral law, adopting the four Confucian virtues as criteria for moral judgment. To sum up, he is for an autonomous and egocentric ethic resting upon the freedom of the will. In passing he recognizes the influence of evolution on morals, but only as regards its frequently injurious effects. The critics have considered this treatise as one of the most searching syntheses in the field of ethics published in China for the past fifty years, and have brought out that its conclusions are in harmony with the theories of Wang Yang-ming and the ideal values.

In these latter years dissertations on ethics have been particularly numerous. One senses from this a reaction against the ever more pronounced leaning towards materialism in intellectual circles. T'ang Chün-i, the Hegelian already cited, is especially concerned with the moral problem. In his *The Establishment of the Moral Self* (道 德 自 我 之 建 立) (1944), he adopts as his method the phenomenology of the mind, gives ten steps to the development of the ego, and shows that ethics starts from the individual instinct, to develop into a transcendental ethic. Along the way he examines the moral ideal which animates scholars, artists, moralists, Nietzschean heroes, and Hindu mystics. Finally he comes to the Chinese Confucianists, whom he calls 'the apostles of the sentiment of mercy[34] centred upon man'. Hsieh Yu-wei, as we have seen earlier, has developed similar ideas in his *Elements of Ethics* (倫 理 學 大 綱). He adopts in part the theories of Royce and Bradley on moral judgment and freedom, in order to refute utilitarianism; but he bases himself also on a Confucianist syncretism. In order to show the connection between freedom and self-realization he says: 'Freedom is the faculty of the "self" for self-determination, for self-realization. I call true "self" the ideal self. This self is not other than at one with nature and the universe, with morals, with law. Thus natural law, moral law, and judicial law are the natural law, the moral law, and the judicial law of the self. By respecting these laws in my conduct I respect the nature of my authentic self. But to know one's nature and be true to it, is in all of one's actions to imitate the bird that flies and the fish that swims—which is what the *Chung Yung* (*Doctrine of the Mean*) calls "following Nature". Now to follow nature is freedom; not to conform to it, is non-freedom.'[35]

The moralists and the surrounding pessimism

The flourishing of these manuals on ethics, as we have said, is a reaction against materialism; it shows the disquietude and disorder of many minds. Certain authors, as after the War of 1914–18, impute to materialism all the misfortunes of mankind. Lin Yutang, the celebrated essayist, who not long ago vaunted his Epicurean positivism, has more recently made some astonishing declarations in his *Between Tears and Laughter* (1943), which are contrary to his beliefs of yesteryear. 'Modern thought is materialistic to the marrow of its bones. This materialism is the incentive for nine out of ten of our actions; in fact, it clouds our minds. Truly the worship of matter is excessive.'[36] 'Man is nothing but an atom in a machine which turns without end.'[37] And he advocates the return to spiritual values. This complaint was echoed by Lo Chia-lun—a professor named by the Nationalist Government to the post of ambassador to the Indies—in his book, *A New Conception of Life* (新人生觀) (1942). 'We live in a strange world. On the one hand immense progress, on the other pitiless destruction; here very precise knowledge, there disordered action. The forces of religion, of morals, of authority, have collapsed. The old beliefs have gone and the new ones are not yet established. Hence it results that man is sunk in perplexity, scepticism, the negation of everything, and in consequence he suffers the emptiness of life.'[38] The author seeks the remedy for this radical pessimism in the restoring to favour of the virtues of faith, zeal, and conviction in an intellectual ideal, one which can give a strong incentive to action. This he explains in detail in the course of his book. A third writer, Fu T'ung-hsien, begins with these words in the preface of his book *Philosophy and Life*: 'At present we live in an extremely troubled period. Everything is unstable . . . and, because everything is unstable, man is easily inclined to let himself go. . . . One says to oneself, today I am alive, but tomorrow I don't know if I shall continue to be; so it is better to enjoy myself to the maximum.' Ho Lin notes the persistence of pessimism even after the victory over Japan, and seeks to revive the morale of the nation: 'We wish that the ideas contained in these essays may correct the prevailing apathetic, depressed psychology.'[39] At the same date, a young thinker fresh from college, Chang Hsin-i, tells how the world-wide catastrophes of perpetual wars spurred his interest in philosophy: 'In 1935, I was studying in the department of physics at Tsinghua University. One winter's evening the sound of artillery-fire made me reflect. . . . All the countries of the world are preparing for war. . . . Thinking of the misfortunes of mankind, I felt vague seethings in my heart. . . . I mused that mankind has had thousands of years of civilization, that it has produced innumerable sages, heroes, and geniuses. Why then have they not been able to deliver the world from the evils which overwhelm it? . . . I finally came to a conclusion: the world's misfortunes arise from the fact that man's sciences are too young.' These lines, used in the preface, justify the title of the book, *The Philosophy of a New World* (新 世 界 的 哲 學).[40] The author set himself from that time to study philosophy and the 'sciences of man', that is to say, psychology, statistics, economics, politics, law, and sociology; and he devised a system composed of three elements, pragmatism as the method, 'Mo Ti-ism' as the ethic, and tridemism as the political philosophy. It is clear that all these systems of morals stem in large part from the anguish arising out of contemporary circumstances.

Tendencies in psychology

In psychology the dominant school is that of behaviourism, thanks in great part to Kuo Jen-yüan, the principal specialist in questions of psychology; but many other authors have expounded the same thesis. Freudian psychoanalysis has also attracted much attention from the scholars, although to a lesser degree. Abnormal psychology has been studied by the great aesthetician Chu Kuang-ch'ien, of whom we shall speak in the following section. Educational psychology, especially child psychology, has been studied a great deal, Shu Hsin-ch'eng being one who has done a great deal in this field, publishing many works.

We shall not dwell at all on psychology, which is in China more a science than a division of philosophy. In the Chinese catalogues psychology appears among the natural sciences under the same heading as anthropology. Now we shall come to the last division of philosophy which we have not yet treated, aesthetics.

Chu Kuang-ch'ien and aestheticism

We have mentioned earlier the first of the modern aestheticians, Ts'ai Yüan-p'ei, and discussed his theory of art as the substitute for religion. His thesis did not lack for response. In 1928 a certain Hsü Ch'ing-yü published a *Philosophy of Beauty* (美 的 哲 學), in which he discussed aesthetic problems. He treated at length the theories of Confucius on music and the *Odes*, and finally took up again the question posed by Ts'ai Yüan-p'ei: can art replace religion?[41]

Taken from this angle aesthetics had little chance of drawing the attention of many thinkers in our positivistic century. But by shifting the problem a little—that is to say, by comparing aesthetics not with religion but with ethics—the philosophy of beauty provoked a great deal of interest among the moderns. An idea which was particularly widespread due to its attractiveness for many people, was the conception of the life 'of truth, beauty and goodness'. By these terms it was meant that the aim of life is the search for truth, or scientific culture, for good, or moral culture, and for beauty, or aesthetic culture. And generally among these three values, first place was given to the idea of beauty, as we have seen with Fu T'ung-hsien; from which it is understandable that some were tempted to sublimate it to the point of comparing it with religion. Such an attitude was very widespread. Thus, Hsü Chih-mo, the foremost Chinese poet of the present century said: 'There is no better means of attaining to the good than by way of the beautiful; our aesthetic intuition is a much surer criterion than our instinct, our moral sense.'[42] The essayist and humorist, Lin Yutang, has echoed the same sentiment. Another writer, Feng Tzu-k'ai (also a talented cartoonist), likewise applied himself to theoretical beauty, treating the question *ex professo* in several of his works. Thus in *Artistic Taste* (藝 術 趣 味) (1934), he lays it down that art is not a mere craft or technique, but a superior activity of man which expresses a transcendent world; for in the grasping of beauty the eyes of the soul are more important than the eyes of the body. 'Intellectual research proves the desire to create truth. One tries in his conduct to create goodness. One cultivates art by desiring to create beauty. To bring about a better, truer, and more beautiful world, is the goal of human life. Unfortunately man's understanding of beauty is far from equalling his comprehension regarding truth and goodness. And yet if man cannot perfect his aesthetic culture, he cannot expand his "personality".'[43] He concludes: 'Aesthetic education is a very profound education of the heart which is bound to affect all of life.'[44]

These three men are only writers and should not detain us here. Let us turn now to the philosophers who have derived systems of aesthetic thought from these theories. In 1944, Ch'en Chu-shan published *The Art of Living* (人 生 藝 術), in which he builds up an ethic based on the 'transcendental good'. He begins by noting that the 'aesthetic conception of life is a very current expression today'. However, personally he intends to write a work which is not speculative, but practical, ethical, in bringing together the concepts of 'life' and 'art'. 'In my opinion,' he says, 'Life is comparable to a harmonious and complex symphony. If one considered it only in its isolated aspects, each dissociated from the others, it would seem as monotonous as the sound of the bonze striking on the wooden fish.'[45] How can we arrive at the synthesis of all its aspects? By the union of three elements, the true, the good, and the beautiful. 'The art of living that we advocate is an art formed by the synthesis of truth, goodness, and beauty, and not art in general, which is confined to only the aesthetic side.'[46] The three values of truth, goodness, and beauty correspond respectively to the three faculties of man, intellect, will, and feeling; and they are attained only if one follows the 'path' or 'ideal', which is to say, the principles of the art of living. These principles are the essence of the Confucian ethic, and they postulate various methods for cultivating the intellect, the will, and the feelings, and for realizing such harmonious concord within the family, the nation, and the international domain as will lead to the Great Concord. In short his aesthetic ethic almost comprises the Confucian ideal.

But the great master of aestheticism is Chu Kuang-ch'ien. After 1929 he enjoyed a lively success through his little book *Twelve Letters to the Young* (給青年的 十 二 封 信), which ran to more than thirty editions. He counselled young people unpretentiously on their private life, their student life, and their social life. He said particularly: 'When our efforts are crowned with success, we should bend our energies to the triumph of the real. But when our force proves insufficient, it is then necessary to leave the real temporarily. The life of artists is an evasion: works of art help us to flee reality and offer us consolation in the world of the ideal.'[47] Such was the *leitmotif* of his subsequent works. The mere enumeration is suggestive enough of it: *The Psychology of Literary Art* (文 藝 心 理 學) (1936), *On Beauty* (談 美) (1932), and *On Poetry* (詩 論) (1948). But above all he is the great specialist on Benedetto Croce, whose *Principles of Esthetics* he translated as (美 學 原 理)[48] and about whom he wrote a *Critique of the Philosophy of Croce* (克 羅 齊 哲 學 評 述) (1948). Although by and large he follows the ideas of the Italian philosopher, he diverges from him on many points.

His central thought is well expressed by this passage, taken from the conclusion of one of his books: 'All life is a work of art in the large sense. . . . A perfect life has the beauties of a literary composition of superior value. . . . It is the expression of a personality. Most people imagine that the artist is a man without trammels, following his fancies. That is false. In whatever concerns art, the artist is very serious. . . . Such a poet will erase ten times before finding the definitive word. Those who love life should do the same. Hence, in advocating the artistic conception of life, we declare the austerity of life.'[49] In other words the author, who has read all the theories of 'beauty' from Plato to Croce, going by way of Kant and Hegel, comes to the conclusion that the highest form of practical morals is artistic activity, since the summit of 'supreme good' and 'absolute beauty' coincide. Rejecting the idea of a transcendent Being, he reserves to the concept of 'beauty' a higher place than the concepts of 'truth' and 'goodness'. For him, aesthetics is above ethics; it seems to him more spiritual, more beautifying. Here is how he transposes this speculative conception into his attitude on practical life: 'I often doubt philosophical systems, but I love to study them, for I find charm in them. The theories of scholars can move my soul as much as the Venus de Milo or the Ninth Symphony. The more profound the delight experienced, the more life is beautiful and full. The artistic conception of life is the delighting in life. When this delight exists, man is like a free and happy spirit.'[50]

One might be tempted to believe that the domain of aesthetics is at the antipodes of Marxist preoccupations, for the literary history of modern China still resounds to their maledictions on the partisans of 'art for art's sake'. However, the Marxist school tries to enter into all sections of culture, including aesthetics. After the victory in 1945 a till then unknown author, Ts'ai I, undertook a theoretical study of arts and aesthetics through a series of works such as *The New Esthetics* (新美學) (1948), and *The Sociology of Art* (藝術社會學).[51] In the same collection other authors worked from the same angle, some with original works, some with translations. Kuo Mo-jo republished *A Century of Archaeological Discoveries in the Fine Arts* by Michaelis. Others translated the biographies of celebrated artists such as Tschaikovsky, Picasso, Michelangelo, Taine, and Stravinsky. One of them, a certain Hu Man, even wrote a *History of the Fine Arts in China* (中國美術史) (1942), entirely dominated by the same prejudices. In the preface he admonishes the reader in these words: 'Art, in the past, was based on the exploitation of the people, the workers: it is now a question therefore of restoring to the common masses their artistic heritage.' And some lines later he adds, if possible even more clearly: 'The contents of the present book rest on the suggestions furnished by the doctrine of the New Democracy.'

Of this group of Marxist authors Ts'ai I is incontestably the principal theoretician, the philosopher. Let us follow him in his *New Aesthetics*, written in 1944 and published in 1948. He begins by declaring that the old aesthetics, having shown its contradictions, should be thrown out and replaced. The error of the past has been to consider art as the basis of aesthetics; at the two poles of thought the subjectivists and the objectivists have erred equally on this point. The truth is completely opposite. 'I teach that the beautiful is an objective reality, that the beauty of objective reality is the source of the aesthetic sense and of artistic beauty. Consequently the path of exact aesthetics is to observe the beautiful, to grasp the nature of the beautiful in things, that is, the real.'[52] From this basis the author attempts to demolish step by step the conceptions of Chu Kuang-ch'ien, whose school he scornfully calls that of subjective beauty, of aesthetics based upon metaphysics; and he believes he can give this definition: 'The beautiful is the manifestation of the universal character of the species in the particular. . . . Beautiful beings are the typical beings, because in them the truth and the nature of reality appears more plainly expressed.'[53] But since individual beings evolve ceaselessly just like the species, there can be no question of absolute, eternal beauty.

In a little different spirit than the pure aestheticians and Ts'ai Yüan-p'ei in particular, Wu Mi declares that the artistic feeling and the religious sentiment are not opposed, but mutually complement each other. 'Both of them', he says, 'permit men to find happiness by suppressing sorrow, by going beyond the fetters of matter, of the world, in order to penetrate into the ideal domain of the spirit. As for their relationship, it is that of ends and means: the religious spirit is the end, the cultivation of art is the means. Religion is comparable to the fruit, art to the flower. In ordinary life a man who has not received the baptism of art is like a prisoner in a dark prison. Religious spirit and artistic cultivation complement and are indispensable to each other. In antiquity, in the Orient as in the Occident, the greatest art is founded on the religious spirit, which activates great epochs and great talents. If one wishes to reach the sanctuary of religion, the best means is to penetrate it by the cultivation of art.'[54] Many of the ideas put forth by Wu Mi are akin to the system of Ts'ai Yüan-p'ei, in particular the conception of aesthetics as the source of religion. But Wu Mi intended to make aesthetics only an adjunct to religion, not a substitute for it. Still more, he wanted the religious spirit to animate our modern democracies and our industrialized society. Many of his theories are borrowed from the religious sociology of Max Weber, from the American humanism of Irving Babbit and Paul E. Moore and, finally, from the book by Hoernlé, *God, Spirit, Life, Matter*, of which he published a translation with commentary. This book explained the tendency of the sciences and of modern philosophy to 'revolt against matter'—to use his own expression.

Hung Ch'ien, interpreter of the Vienna school (Moritz Schlick and R. Carnap).

Finally, one can also add to the aesthetic current a new philosophical school which has flourished in Europe for more than ten years under the name, 'the Vienna school'. A certain number of authors have endeavoured to construct an aesthetic logic which envisages denying all value to metaphysics and reducing it to the role of a 'mere poetry of concepts'. According to them the only merit of metaphysics is to enrich our inner life and develop our world of experience; but it cannot increase the world of knowledge. Metaphysics is no more than a literary phenomenon like poetry: it does not in the least contribute to the quest for truth. Arguing from this the attempt is made to construct a philosophy on other bases: a logical base and a practical base, that of a philosophy of life. The logical aspect of this philosophy has been developed in China by Wang Hsien-chün and Hu Shih-hua. The practical aspect, on the other hand, has been brought out by Hung Ch'ien, a former student in Vienna, and a fervent admirer of the great master of the school. Hung Ch'ien has given a general introduction to it in his work, *The Philosophy of the Vienna School* (維 也 納 學 派 哲 學).[55] The professor, he says, is rich in poetic sentiments, but to his great regret has never been able to become a poet, so he is wont to say: 'We are all repressed poets.' Hence he considers life from the same angle as the poet Schiller: 'It is only when man is taking recreation that he is perfect.' This term 'recreation', or 'diversion', must suggest the idea not of bagatelles to kill time, but of activity undertaken by the disinterested free play of the will, without the preoccupation of a set aim. For him all knowledge is the product of 'recreations' or 'diversions' of the human spirit. The understanding of all culture lies there. Fung Yu-lan, having explained these principles in one of his recent books, *New Wisdom* (新 知 言) (1946), accepted certain of these ideas, while also criticizing them. On the whole he has a high estimation of the Vienna school. That did not prevent his being taken vigorously to task by Hung Ch'ien, who criticized his metaphysics as being devoid of meaning or depth, of not being capable of touching the heart like the traditional metaphysics which was so rich in poetry. This was the signal for an argument between the two philosophers, which was joined by Chin Yüeh-lin and Shen Yu-ting.

In short the philosophy of the Vienna school has elicited great interest in Chinese intellectual circles. In our opinion the reason for this vogue is in large part due to its conception of life, rather than to its logical aspect—that is to say to its theory of disinterested activity of the spirit—and to its attacks against the dogmatism of metaphysics.

1. Chan Wen-hu, *The Epistemological Pluralism of Chang Tung-sun* 張 東 蓀 的 多 元 認 識 論 , pp. 88–9. *Tr. note:* This work is not listed in the Bibliography.
2. Chang Tung-sun, *New Philosophical Theories* 新 哲 學 論, 1929, p. 24.
3. *Tr. note:* No citation is given for the foregoing quotation.
4. Chang Tung-sun, *op. cit.*, p. 62.
5. Chang Tung-sun, *Moral Philosophy* 道 德 哲 學 , 1930, p. 600.
6. *Times and Culture Magazine* 時 與 文 , April 11, 1947, n.p.
7. *ibid.*, May 30, 1945, n.p.
8. Chang Tung-sun, *Reason and Democracy* 理 性 與 民 主 , 1946, p. 178.
9. Chang Tung-sun, *Democracy and Socialism* 民 主 主 義 與 社 會 主 義 , 1947, p. 72.
10. *ibid.*, p. 73.
11. Ho Lin, *Contemporary Chinese Philosophy* 當 代 中 國 哲 學 , 1941, p. 39.
12. *ibid.*, p. 48.
13. Fu T'ung-hsien, *Philosophy and Life* 哲 學 與 人 生 , 1947, p. 243.
14. Fu T'ung-hsien, *Outline of Esthetics* 美 學 綱 要 , 1948, p. 124.
15. Li Ta, *Elements of Sociology*, pp. 845–6. *Tr. note:* This work is not listed in the Bibliography, but the second half, issued afterwards as *Modern Sociology* 現 代 社 會 學 (1947), is listed.
16. *ibid.*, p. 854.
17. *Tr. note:* However, in the Bibliography, the author has given the date of publication of the *Philosophy of the People* as 1934.
18. Ai Ssu-ch'i, *Philosophy of the People* 大 眾 哲 學 , 1934, p. 9.
19. *Tr. note: loc. cit.?* (No citation is given by author.)
20. T'an Fu-chih, *Philosophical Critiques* 哲 學 批 判 集 , 1937, p. 185.

21. *Tr. note:* This is the author's translation. A closer rendering would be 'The Bookstore of Arduous (Mental) Ploughing'.

22. Yeh Ch'ing, *Problems of Philosophy* 哲 學 問 題 , 1936, p. 269.

23. Cited by Huang T'e, *The Weapon of Criticism* 批 判 的 武 器 , 1941, p. 166.

24. *Tr. note:* No dates of publication are given, either here or in the Bibliography.

25. Ho Lin, *Contemporary Chinese Philosophy* 當 代 中 國 哲 學 , 1941. Appendix by Hsieh Yu-wei, p. 147.

26. Fung Yu-lan, *Supplement to the History of Chinese Philosophy* 中 國 哲 學 史 補 , Appendix, 'Why China Has No Science' (in English), pp. 36 and 39.

27. *Tr. note:* This work is not listed in the Bibliography.

28. Kuo Chan-po, *History of Chinese Thought during the Past Fifty Years* 近 五 十 年 中 國 思 想 史 , 1935, p. 314.

29. Cited by Yeh Ch'ing, in the review *New China* 新 中 華 , vol. II, no. 24, December 25, 1934: 'Criticism of Li Shih-ts'en'.

30. Chang Tung-sun, *Moral Philosophy* 道 德 哲 學 , 1930, p. 560.

31. Ho Lin, *Contemporary Chinese Philosophy* 當 代 中 國 哲 學 , 1941, p. 60.

32. *loc. cit.*

33. In the bibliographical review, *New Books Monthly* 新 書 月 刊, no. 1, October 1948.

34. *Tr. note: pitié*—one assumes the Chinese is *jen* 仁 .

35. Ho Lin, *op. cit.*, p. 56.

36. Lin Yutang, *Between Tears and Laughter* 啼 笑 皆 非 , 1943, p. 64. *Tr. note:* As the author gives Chinese characters for this title, presumably he used a Chinese translation, although this book was originally written in English.

37. *ibid.*, p. 182.

38. Lo Chia-lun, *A New Conception of Life* 新 人 生 觀 , 1942, p. 105.

39. Ho Lin, *Culture and Life* 文 化 與 人 生 , 1947, Preface, p. 2.

40. *Tr. note:* This work is not listed in the Bibliography.

41. *Tr. note:* The answer: no. (See Bibliography, author's note *re* this book.)

42. Hsü Chih-mo, in *Creation Magazine* 創 造 , vol. II, August 25, 1929: 'Art and Life'.
43. Feng Tzu-k'ai, *Artistic Taste* 藝 術 趣 味 , n.d., p. 6.
44. *ibid.*, p. 38.
45. Ch'en Chu-shan, *The Art of Living* 人 生 藝 術 , 1944, p. 6. *Tr. note:* This refers to the block which the bonzes strike while chanting. (Presumably the sentence in quotation marks above this one is from the same passage, but no citation has been given by author.)
46. *ibid.*, p. 16.
47. Chu Kuang-ch'ien, *Twelve Letters to the Young* 給 青 年 的 十 二 封 信 , n.d., p. 97. *Tr. note:* This work is not listed in the Bibliography.
48. *Tr. note:* This work is listed in the Bibliography, but no date of publication is given.
49. Chu Kuang-ch'ien, *On Beauty* 談 美 , 1932, pp. 128 and 132.
50. *ibid.*, p. 136.
51. *Tr. note:* According to the Bibliography, this latter is a new translation of a work by Friche; no date of publication is given.
52. Ts'ai I, *The New Esthetics* 新 美 學 , 1948, p. 17.
53. *ibid.*, p. 80.
54. Cited in Ho Lin, *Contemporary Chinese Philosophy* 當 代 中 國 哲 學 , 1941, p. 64.
55. *Tr. note:* This work is listed in the Bibliography, but no date of publication is given.

CONCLUSION

AFTER having travelled through the maze of these disparate systems, it is fitting to collect our thoughts in order to clarify the essential ideas which have been accepted in the intellectual world of China and have become, so to speak, current money in public opinion.

Up to this point we have placed the mass of thinkers in two camps: the 'Orientalists' and the 'Occidentalists'. Although this distinction should not be pressed too far, since a certain number of authors derive their inspiration as much from one side as the other, it does correspond all the same to a reality. For a good part the history of modern thought in China is the confronting of Oriental philosophies with the Occidental systems, and this unending comparison leads the authors to declare themselves, to choose between the two metaphysics.

The term 'Orientalists', according to our definition, designates, therefore, the intelligentsia who remain faithful to the national tradition on the whole. All moreover agree in admitting that there are things to be changed, that it is necessary to introduce the sciences and methods of the Occident; but having made this concession they sing with all their strength the spiritual superiority of the Orient. Although they appreciate the benefits of science, they point out the catastrophes it has brought to the world, especially after the war of 1914. Also they retain their sympathy and admiration for the moral philosophy of Confucianism, and they gladly believe that China has its word to say in world civilization through the instrumentality of this ancient ideal with its still recognizable values. From the philosopher Liang Shu-ming to the statesmen, the heads of the Kuomintang, they preach the traditional Confucian virtues of 'benevolence' and 'sincerity'. To tell the truth, they often create an eclectic system, metaphysically and ethically based on Confucianism, but adopting the method, the logic, and the new concepts of the Occident. Even though they modernize the national cultural heritage, they themselves remain faithful to their general spirit, that is to say, to the stress put on the spirit, on ideals, and on liberty. They remain moralists above all. Metaphysics has meaning for them only as a foundation for ethics.

From this stemmed their lamentations after World War II, as they noted the collapse of ideals, the spiritual disquietude, the disorder.

Naturally they want to find in Occidental idealism, in its most authoritative representatives, arguments to support their beliefs. They go to Bergson, Hegel, Bradley and Royce, sometimes also to Kant or Plato, in order desperately to attempt to oppose the growing materialism. Be they Confucianists, Buddhists or vitalists, they never lift themselves beyond rationalism, for even Buddhist philosophy has always been resolutely atheistic. In politics they generally represent the 'right', conservative, 'feudal' thought—the past, to use the words of their adversaries.

The 'Occidentalists' on the contrary are characterized by their rupture with tradition, and their worship of science and sociology. After 1911, they cried, 'Long live science and democracy!' That was the slogan underscored by all the periodicals. But since 1929 or 1930 the pole of opinion has been displaced somewhat, and now the intellectuals think especially of the social realities, and subordinate science to that. All the modern literature is dominated by this concern. The development of the social sciences has made unheard-of progress. As early as 1931 a chronicler notes that according to the results of his inquiry thirty per cent of the books being published dealt with the social sciences in the large sense and for the most part expounded the theses and principles of Marxist socialism. Since then this movement has not slackened in the least, despite the coercive measures adopted by the Nationalist government; and, following the Pacific war, the proportion appeared to be yet larger. Not all of these authors who extol the theories of Marx necessarily belong to the Communist Party. Many, if not the greater number, remained outside of it, be it because they were opposed to violent methods, or because they only adopted the dialectical method of thought without accepting its extreme consequences, or for reasons of which we are not aware. The Marxist group was at all times the most influential, the most active, the most prolific in the world of ideas. Alongside of them are the positivists or mechanistic materialists, as the preceding (who call themselves 'scientific materialists') scornfully call them. These positivists also blindly believe that 'science' equals 'materialism', and reject all absolute values which do not fall under scientific determinism. For all of them religion has been decidedly banished by science, so much so that they are persuaded that science and religion are two contradictory notions; and while they still believe in the existence of ethics, they subordinate it to sociology or science. They no longer admit of an absolute, invariable ethic, and content themselves with a relative ethic adapted to the circumstances of time and place. Scientific or social facts preoccupy them. They no longer pronounce the name of 'morals', but speak of the 'conception of life', which seems more modern, less reactionary, more scientific. And because they hold logic in high esteem they study all the methodologies which have been current in the Occident. The method most in favour is obviously the Marxist dialectic, after which come the pragmatic method of Dewey, the Russellian logic and others, the logic of the Vienna school coming latest in date. However, none of them disown the past. They study it a great deal. Even the Marxist authors attempt to re-evaluate the ancient philosophy of China: only they apply themselves to these studies with a preconceived aim, for they claim to find among their ancients the beginnings of materialism, pragmatism and socialism. They do not wish to reject all tradition, but to insufflate it with a new spirit, the spirit of modern Occidental civilization. This is the import of the polemic against Confucianism of 1915 to 1920, of the debate on the cultures of Orient and Occident of 1922, and finally of the discussion aroused by the manifesto 'on the culture suitable to China' of 1935. These 'Occidentalists', who represent the scientific and socialistic current, are in the main the 'progressives', the political 'left'.

In reality it is necessary to keep from systematizing too much. Among the 'Orientalists' one also encounters the positivistic element, as, for example, Fung Yu-lan. Likewise, among the 'Occidentalists' there are sometimes idealists. But, while not claiming it to be any more than a general tendency, it cannot be denied that in practice 'Orientalist' is equivalent to idealist, as 'Occidentalist' is synonymous with materialist.

And now this party of the intelligentsia, which has worked with all its might for the triumph of the new ideas, sees dawning before it the day so long desired. The old philosophical societies have obviously gone down in the fray: another has taken their place, 'The Association of Marxist Intellectual Workers'. What will it be able to add to the mass of materialist productions which is already so imposing? One wonders. Has not everything already been said? Despite the efforts of the Nationalist government, all the classical Marxist works had already been translated into Chinese, sometimes by three or four different authors. Is there anything left to philosophy but to veil its face? Was Yeh Ch'ing right in prophesying its decease? Only the future can tell.

APPENDIX

REPRESENTATIVE BIBLIOGRAPHY
OF AUTHORS AND PRINCIPAL WORKS
OF THE LAST FIFTY YEARS
1900–1950

CONTENTS

NOTE

As indicated by the title this bibliography is by no means intended to be exhaustive, but only to be representative of the best authors and their best works. Authors are classified according to subject-matter, the first under each heading being ordinarily the most representative. Publishers (most of which are in Shanghai) are indicated by numerals in bold-faced type, according to the list which follows the bibliography. Chinese characters for authors, as well as dates (wherever possible), may be found by consulting the Index of Authors. (The reader is cautioned that works by a particular author may frequently be found under more than one heading.)

GENERAL HISTORIES

Kuo Chan-po, *History of Chinese Thought during the Past Fifty Years* 近 五 十 年 中 國 思 想 史 , **8**, 1935; 431 pp. The author analyses the writings of some twenty thinkers, beginning with K'ang Yu-wei, describes the movement of thought (controversies and schools) and the introduction of Occidental systems.

Ho Lin, *Contemporary Chinese Philosophy* 當 代 中 國 哲 學 , **9**, 1945; 155 pp. About half of this book is taken up with a general survey of philosophical writings; the other half deals with various movements of thought, and with a discussion of the question of knowledge versus action.

THE PRECURSORS OF CONTEMPORARY THOUGHT

K'ang Yu-wei, *The One World* (literally, as rendered by author, *The Book of the Great Concord*) 大 同 書 , **2**, 1935 (only complete edition); 452 pp. A mass of theories borrowed from Confucianism, socialism, evolutionism. A very audacious work which was very influential.

T'an Ssu-t'ung, *Theory of Jen* 仁 學 , in *T'an Ssu-t'ung Anthology* 譚 嗣 同 集 , **55**, 1928; 97 pp. The author was a disciple of K'ang Yu-wei, and a martyr in the 'Hundred Days of Reform'. His book is a blend of neo-Confucian, Buddhist, Christian, anti-Manchu, and new-Western ideas. *Jen* is equated with 'ether', but is a moral as well as a spiritual concept.

Chang T'ai-yen, *General Discussion of Sinology* 國 學 概 論, 2. Studies on the Chinese Classics.

Liang Ch'i-ch'ao (Jen-kung), *History of the Evolution of Chinese Scholarship* 中 國 學 術 思 想 變 遷 史, 10.

2. *General Discussion of Ch'ing Dynasty Scholarship* 清 代 學 術 概 論, 1, 1921; 183 pp.

3. *Complete Essays of the Yin Ping Shih* 飲 冰 室 全 集, 2, 1902 (most recent edition, 2, 1949). Essays on civilization and various modern theories—which the author criticizes.

4. *Anthology of Liang Jen-kung's Lectures on Scholarship* 梁 任 公 學 術 講 演 集, 1, two series, 1923 and 1925. Further critiques of modern thought.

5. *Liang Jen-kung's Recent Writings, First Series* 梁 任 公 近 著 第 一 集, 1, 1925. In three parts: Impressions of Europe, Studies on the Buddhist Classics, and Essays on Sinology and Politics. Many sound ideas, and very influential at one time; but now quite *passé*.

THE SPECIALISTS IN TRADITIONAL CHINESE PHILOSOPHY

Fung Yu-lan, *History of Chinese Philosophy* 中 國 哲 學 史

1. Volume One 1931, new edition in two volumes 1934; 1040 pp. The authority in the field to date. It has been criticized as giving a too positivistic interpretation of ancient philosophy. (For English translation, see translator's bibliography.)

2. *New Li Hsüeh* 新 理 學, 1, 1939; 312 pp. *Li Hsüeh* is translated by E. R. Hughes as 'dogma of the ideal pattern', and by Fr. Brière as 'the norm'. This book modernizes the positivistic Confucianism of Chu Hsi, while still following it rather closely. It is the personal metaphysical system of Fung Yu-lan, an adaptation and blending of Chinese traditional philosophy with Occidental thought.

3. *New Realities* 新事論 , 1, 1940; 230 pp. Seeks a solution to the new practical problems of China in political, social, cultural, and other areas, whence its sub-title, 'China's Road to Freedom'.

4. *Counsels for the New Age* 新世訓 , 5, 1940; 198 pp. The author's philosophy of life, a Confucian rationalism.

5. *New Treatise on the Nature of Man* 新原人 , 1, 1943; 147 pp. Treats of problems 'not touched upon in the three preceding', says the author in his preface—problems of life.

6. *New Treatise on the Nature of Tao* 新原道 , 1, 1945; 123 pp. Retraces the principal currents of traditional Chinese thought so as to indicate the position of neo-Confucianism, which is the author's own school. Described by the author as a supplement to his two-volume history (1) above. (For English translation, see translator's bibliography.)

7. *New Wisdom* 新知言 , 1, 1946; 104 pp. The contents are indicated by the author's own English title for this work, *New Treatise on the Methodology of Metaphysics*. The neo-Confucian methodology is compared with that of Plato, Spinoza, Kant, etc.

Liang Shu-ming, *The Civilizations of Orient and Occident and Their Philosophies* 東西文化及其哲學 , 1, 1922; 216 pp.

2. *Writings of Shu-ming before Thirty* 漱溟卅前文錄 , 1, 1930. Various studies on cultural, moral, and pedagogical problems.

3. *Writings of Shu-ming after Thirty* 漱溟卅後文錄 , 1, 1930. Especially concerned with criticizing Occidental education. Corrects the excessively anti-Western position of (1) above.

4. *Writings on Education* 教育文錄 , 11, 1935. Disquisition on education *à propos* of the author's experiences at the Institute of Rural Reconstruction in Chouping, Shantung. Confucian in ethical outlook.

Chang Chün-mai (Carson Chang), *Science and the Philosophy of Life* 科學與人生觀, 12, 1925. A compilation of the author's lectures advocating a free, autonomous ethic in opposition to determinism. It was these lectures which gave rise to one of the liveliest philosophical controversies of the period.

2. Joad's *Spirit and Matter* (translation) 心 與 物 , 1.

3. H. Driesch's *The Relativity of Einstein and Its Critics* (translation) 愛 因 斯 坦 相 對 論 及 其 批 評 , 1. The translator has borrowed many elements from Driesch and Bergson to support his own Confucian idealism.

4. Fichte's *Letters to the German Nation* (translation) 菲 希 特 對 德 意 志 國 民 講 演 , 1.

Hsieh Wu-liang, *History of Chinese Philosophy* 中 國 哲 學 史 , 2. One of the principal works in the field.

2. *Philosophy of Wang Ch'ung* 王 充 哲 學 , 2. This philosopher of the Latter Han Dynasty (he lived A.D. 27–*ca.* 97) is here studied for his political theories.

3. *The Chu Hsi School* 朱 子 學 派 , 2. This Confucian school is rationalistic and positivistic. (Chu Hsi: A.D. 1130–1200.)

Chung T'ai, *History of Chinese Philosophy* 中 國 哲 學 史 , 1.

2. *Supplement to Hsün Tzu Annotated* 荀 注 訂 補 , 1. (Hsün Tzu: died *ca.* 238 B.C.)

Chiang Wei-ch'iao, *Outline History of Chinese Philosophy* 中 國 哲 學 史 綱 要 , 2, 1934–35, in three volumes.

2. *History of Chinese Philosophy during the Last Three Hundred Years* 中 國 近 三 百 年 哲 學 史 , 2, 1932.

3. *The Philosophies of Yang Chu and Mo Ti* 楊 墨 哲 學 , 1. Yang Chu was a hedonist (?fourth century B.C.). Mo Ti (*ca.* 479–381 B.C.) advocated utilitarianism and universal love, and was the greatest opponent of Mencius.

Ch'en Chu, *The I Ching in Sum* 周 易 論 略 , 1. The *I Ching* is one of the canonical books. Its title, *Classic of Changes*, refers to its subject matter which is concerned with the interpretation and divination of certain diagrams which are supposed to include in themselves all possible combinations of changes in the universe.

2. *The Chung Yung Annotated and Collated* 中 庸 注 系 , I.
The *Chung Yung* is one of the 'Four Books' of the neo-
Confucian canon; its title means something like the 'golden
mean'.

3. *Lao Tzu* 老 子 , I. Lao Tzu is the first Taoist philosopher
and reputed author of the *Tao Te Ching*, which advocates
naturalism and nihilism. He is supposed to have been an older
contemporary of Confucius, but this is doubtful.

4. *Ten Essays on Moism* 墨 學 十 論 , I.
Ch'ien Mu, *Chinese Confucian Thought* 中 國 儒 家 思 想 ,
13.

(Translator's note: Prof. Ch'ien informs me he has not written
a book by this title; however, the title and publisher may serve
to identify the work to some reader, so this item has been retained here.)

2. *General Discussion of Sinology* 國 學 概 論 , I.

3. *Essentials of the Lun Yü* 論 語 要 略, I. The *Lun Yü* is
generally rendered in English as *The Analects* of Confucius.

4. *Wang Shou-jen* 王 守 仁 , I. This famous opponent of
Chu Hsi, who is the founder of the idealistic school of neo-
Confucianism, is better known by his literary name, Wang
Yang-ming. He lived from 1472 to 1528.

5. *Mo Tzu* 墨 子 , I.

6. *Hui Shih and Kung-Sun Lung* 惠 施 公 孫 龍 , I.
Two logicians, often called sophists, who lived in the fourth
century B.C.

Hsieh Meng, *Confucius* 孔 子 , I.

2. *The Wang Yang-ming School* 陽 明 學 派, 2.

Ho Lin, *New Essays on Confucian Thought* 儒 家 思 想 新 論
, 3. A symposium of various authors.

2. *The Saying, 'Knowledge Is Difficult, Action is Easy', and the
Saying, 'Knowledge and Action Are One,'* 知 難 行 易 說
與 知 行 合 一 說 , 14, 1943.

(Translator's note: For Hu Shih's writings, see the section on
'Utilitarianism, Pragmatism, Anglo-American neo-Realism'.)

BUDDHIST PHILOSOPHY

T'ai Hsü, *True Theory of Reality* 真現實論 , **2**, 1940; 494 pp.

2. *Philosophy* 哲學 , **6**, 1932; 132 pp. Collection of lectures given by the author on various occasions and on various topics.

3. *A View of the History of Liberty* 自由史觀, **6**, 1932; 70 pp. Combats dogmatism, whether religious or political—the monotheistic religions, imperialism, and communism.

4. *T'ai Hsü's Discourses* 太虛演說集, **6**, 1932; in three volumes. Volume One contains lectures on the Buddhist Law in general, on the philosophical school of 'mere ideation', or 'pure idea', which denies the reality of the external world (211 pp.). Volume Two contains lectures on the relationship of modern civilization and Buddhism (161 pp.). Volume Three contains lectures on Buddhist attitudes towards life (140 pp.).

5. *Writings of the Buddhist Teacher T'ai Hsü* 太虛法師文鈔, **6**. Also in three volumes.

6. *Essentials of Buddhism* 佛乘宗要論 , **6**.

7. *Regulations for the Reformation of the Sangha* 整理僧伽制度 , **6**.

8. *New Theory of Idealism* 唯識新論 , **6**. A new statement of the position of the Buddhist school of pure idealism.

Yin Kuang, *Writings of the Buddhist Teacher Yin Kuang* 印度法師文鈔, **6**. In four volumes. The author was the leader of the conservative wing of Buddhist thought and the great adversary of T'ai Hsü,

Huang Ch'an-hua, *Outline of Philosophy* 哲學綱要 , **1**. Under Buddhist influence.

2. *General Discussion of Buddhism* 佛學概論, **1**.

3. *Main Principles Held by the Various Buddhist Sects* 佛教各宗大意 , **1**. In two volumes.

4. *Introduction to Idealism* 唯識導論 , **6**. Idealism of the Buddhist *wei shih* school.

Chiang Wei-ch'iao, *General Discussion of Buddhism* 佛 學 概 論, 1.

2. *History of Chinese Buddhism* 中 國 佛 教 史, 1. In three volumes.

Hsieh Wu-liang, *Outline of Buddhism* 佛 學 大 綱, 2.

Wang En-yang, *General Discussion of Buddhism* 佛 學 概 論, 6.

2. *Complete Analysis of Idealism* 唯 識 通 論, 6. Idealism of the Buddhist *wei shih* school.

Ou-Yang Chien (Ching-wu), *Buddha's Compassion* 釋 悲, 6.

2. *The Buddhist Law: neither Religion nor Philosophy* 佛 法 非 宗 教 非 哲 學, 6.

3. *Explanation of Idealism* 唯 識 講 義, 6. Idealism of the Buddhist *wei shih* school.

Hsiung Shih-li, *New Treatise on Idealism* 新 唯 識 論, 1, 1944; 358 pp. The most profound exposition of the views of the Buddhist *wei shih* school yet produced in modern China. The author adapts his theories to the present day.

Lü Ch'eng, *How to Study Buddhism* 佛 教 研 究 法, 1.

2. *Outline of Indian Logic* 因 明 綱 要, 1. The author is merely a popularizer.

3. *Brief History of Indian Buddhism* 印 度 佛 教 史略, 1.

Chiang Shao-yüan, McGovern's *Manual of Buddhist Philosophy* (translation) 佛 教 哲 學 通 論, 1.

2. G. F. Moore's *Origin and Growth of Religion* (translation) 宗 教 的 出 生 與 長 成, 1.

Feng Ch'eng-chün, Przyluski's *Buddhist Studies* (translation) 佛 學 研 究, 1.

2. Sylvain Levi's *Asvaghosa, the Sutralamkara and Its Sources* (translation) 大 莊 嚴 經 論 探 源, 1.

3. Sylvain Levi's *The Sixteen Arhats* (translation) 法 住 記 及 所 記 阿 羅 漢 考, 1.

Liang Shu-ming, *General Discussion of Indian Philosophy* 印 度 哲 學 概 論, 1, 1919; 313 pp.

Ting Fu-pao, *The Written Foundations of Buddhism* 佛 教 文

基礎, 15. This author is one of the most prolific popularizers of Buddhism.

Fan Ku-nung, *A Buddhist Catechism* 佛教問答, 6. This author is also a prolific popularizer of Buddhism.

N.B.—Modern Buddhist literature is very abundant. We have listed only the principal authors.

THE PHILOSOPHY OF TRIDEMISM AND VITALISM

Sun Yat-sen (Wen), *On Psychological Reconstruction* 心理建設論, 3, 1918. The most philosophical of the author's works. It is based on the views of Wang Yang-ming, but undertakes to correct them somewhat.

2. *Three Principles of the People* (or, *Tridemism*) 三民主義, 3, 1924. The 'Bible' of the Kuomintang; a collection of Dr. Sun's lectures in rather rough form. (For English translations, see translator's bibliography.)

(Translator's note: The most complete and most recent edition of Dr. Sun's works was published in Taipei, Taiwan, in 1952, by the Central Reform Committee (Kuomintang) 中央改造委員會 (in twelve volumes).)

Chiang Kai-shek, *China's Destiny* 中國之命運, 3 1943. This work by China's wartime leader ran to some 200,000 copies. It came to be the new 'Bible' of the Kuomintang, somewhat displacing the *Three Principles of the People*. (For English translation, see translator's bibliography.)

Ch'en Li-fu, *Vitalism* 唯生論, 3, 1934. Collection of the author's lectures which were designed to furnish a metaphysical foundation for tridemism. (For English translation, see translator's bibliography.)

2. *The Origin of Life* 生之原理, 3, 1944. A continuation of the preceding. Treats of cosmology, as well as of ideals of individual and national life. Its theories are based on Bergson, Driesch, and Confucianism.

Ho Hsing-chih, *Theoretical Foundations of Vitalist Philosophy* 唯生論哲學理論之基礎, 3, 1935. Devotes special attention to the vitalist theory of knowledge, an aspect which had been neglected by Ch'en Li-fu.

Jen Chüeh-wu, *Vitalism and the Historical Conception of the People's Livelihood* 唯生論與民生史觀 , **16**, 1933. Another attempt to bridge the gap between materialism and idealism. The biological viewpoint is stressed, especially that central concept of vitalism, the theory of evolution.

Wang Lung-yü, *System of Vitalist Philosophy* 唯生哲學的體系 , **17**, 1936. In three volumes. Volume One discusses vitalism as the philosophical foundation of tridemism, and compares it with materialism and idealism. Volume Two treats of the vitalists' theories of cosmology, history and society. Volume Three expounds the vitalist philosophy of life and ethics.

Chiang Ching-i, *Political System of Vitalism* 唯生論政治學體系 , **18**.

Huang Wen-shan, *Vitalist Conception of History* 唯生論的歷史觀, **3**, 1935.

UTILITARIANISM, PRAGMATISM, ANGLO-AMERICAN
NEO-REALISM

Yen Fu, Stuart Mill's *On Liberty* (translation) 群己權界論 , **1**.

2. Stuart Mill's *System of Logic* (translation) 穆勒名學 ,
1.

3. Jevons' *Elements of Logic* 名學淺說 ,
(Translator's note: For mention of others of Yen Fu's translations, see the present work, Part I, Section on 'Darwinian and Spencerian Evolutionism'. Incidentally the director of Provincial Taiwan Library at Taipei, Prof. Wu K'o-kang, remarked to the translator at one time that Yen Fu's translations have never been surpassed or even equalled.)

Hu Shih, *Outline of the History of Chinese Philosophy* 中國哲學史大綱 , **1**, 1919. Volume One only. The first study of ancient Chinese philosophy by means of the pragmatic method.

(Translator's note: No further volumes were published; in late 1952 Dr. Hu stated he was at work on materials to complete this work.)

2. *The Development of the Logical Method in Ancient China,* **12,** 1922. The author's doctoral dissertation (in English).

3. *Philosophy of Tai Tung-yüan* 戴東原的哲學 , **1,** 1927. Tai Tung-yüan was one of the most important scholars of the Ch'ing Dynasty. He lived from 1724 to 1777.

4. *The Book of the Prince of Huai Nan* 淮南王書 , **19,** 1931. This book, usually known as *Huai Nan Tzu* 淮南子 , is a compilation of Taoist writings composed at the court of a grandson of the first emperor of the Han Dynasty, in the second century B.C.

5. *Essays of Hu Shih* 胡適文存 , **20,** 1921, 1924, and 1930. In three series of four volumes each. These essays are concerned in good part with ancient Chinese philosophy.

Hsü Ch'ung-ch'ing, Dewey's *Reconstruction in Philosophy* (translation) 哲學之改造 , **1.** Hu Shih and T'ang Yüeh also jointly translated this book.

Liu Po-ming, Dewey's *How We Think* (translation) 思維術 , **2.** The translator served as Dewey's interpreter during his lecture tour in China.

Chang Tai-nien, Dewey's *The Sources of a Science of Education* (translation) 教育科學之泉源 , **8.** While Hu Shih paid attention especially to the American philosopher's methodology, most others have devoted their attention to his educational doctrines.

Chu Ching-nung, Dewey's *The School of Tomorrow* (translation) 明日之學校, **1.**

Chou En-jün, Dewey's *Democracy and Education* (translation) 民本主義與教育 , **1.**

Ch'iu Chin-chang, Dewey's *How We Think* (translation) 思想方法論 , **4.**

2. Creighton and Smart's *Elements of Logic* (translation) 論理學大綱 , **4.**

Meng Hsien-ch'eng, William James' *Pragmatism* (translation) 實用主義 , 1.

T'ang Yüeh, William James' *On Emotion* (translation) 論情緒 , 1. Extracted from James' *Principles of Psychology*.

2. William James' *Thought* (translation) 論思想流 , 1. Another chapter from the *Principles of Psychology*.

3. William James' *The Varieties of Religious Experience* (translation) 宗教經驗之種種 , 1.

Fang Tung-mei, Murray's *Pragmatism* (translation) 實驗主義 , 2.

Yen Chi-ch'eng, Russell's *On Scepticism* (translation) 懷疑論 , 1.

Fu Chung-sun, Russell's *Introduction to Mathematical Philosophy* (translation) 羅素算理哲學 , 1.

Wang Tien-chi, *On Logic and Mathematical Logic* 邏輯與數學邏輯論 , 1.

Liu Ch'i-wei, Russell's *On Education* (translation) 羅素教育論 , 1. This book has had at least three Chinese translations.

Chao Yen, Russell's *Education and the Social Order* (translation) 教育與群治 , 1.

Huang Tzu-t'ung, *Metaphysics* 形而上學 , 4. The author was the principal founder of the review *Philosophical Critique*. (Translator's note: For this review and its importance see the present work, Part I, Section on 'The Chinese Philosophical Society'.)

DIALECTICAL AND HISTORICAL MATERIALISM

Ai Ssu-ch'i, *Philosophy of the People* 大眾哲學 , 21, 1934. A popular presentation of Marxism. Sold in enormous quantities.

2. *On How to Think* 思想方法論 , 21, 1935. Establishes that the only scientific method of thought is the materialistic dialectic.

3. Mitin's *Outline of the New Philosophy* (translation) 新哲學大綱 , 21, 1936. Translation of a Soviet manual on Marxism.

4. *Philosophy and Life* 哲學與生活, **21**, 1937. A collection of 'letters to the reader' expounding various Marxist theories and criticizing the opponents of Marxism.

5. *Practice and Theory* 實踐與理論, **21**, 1939. Similar to the above.

6. *Philosophical Selections* 哲學選輯, **22**, 1939; 542 pp.

7. *Manual of the Scientific Conception of History* 科學歷史觀教程, **22**, 1939. Written in collaboration with Wu Li-p'ing (see below).

Li Ta, *Modern Sociology* 現代社會學, **23**, 1937; 854 pp. In spite of the title, this is a treatise on Marxist philosophy. It includes the following topics: materialistic dialectic, historical materialism, the economic structure, the political structure, and the ideological forms of society.

(Translator's note: See the present work, Part III, Section on 'The Marxists: Li Ta, Ai Ssu-ch'i', for additional information on this work and one related to it which is not listed in this bibliography.)

2. Tymjanski's *Introduction to Dialectical Materialism* (translation) 辯證法唯物論教程, **24**.

3. Corter's *Historical Materialism* (translation) 物史觀解說, **2**.

4. A. Thalaimer's *The Modern Conception of the World* (translation) 現代世界觀, **23**.

Shen Chih-yüan, *Fundamental Questions of Modern Philosophy* 現代哲學的基本問題, **25**, 1936; 138 pp. A small popular work preaching neo-materialism.

2. *Talks on the New Conception of Life* 新人生觀講話, **25**, 1936. Another work of popularization for the young. Attempts to establish a sort of Marxist ethic.

3. *Studies in Contemporary Philosophy* 近代哲學論集, **21**. An anthology.

4. *Dictionary of Terms of the New Philosophy* 新哲學辭典, **24**. Dictionary of Marxist technical terms.

5. *History of Contemporary Dialectic* 近代辯證法史, **25**, 1947.

Hu Sheng, *The New Philosophy's Conception of Life* 新 哲 學 的 人 生 觀 , **25**, 1937; 172 pp. Explanation of Marxist ethic for the young.

2. *Introduction to Dialectical Materialism* 辯 證 法 唯 物 論 入 門 , **26**, 1938; 87 pp. A small manual which boils down the Marxist theories for popular consumption.

3. *First Steps in How to Think* 思 想 方 法 初 步 , **27**, 1934; 72 pp. The methodology is of course the dialectic.

4. *How to Think and How to Read* 思 想 方 法 與 讀 書 方 法 , **28**, 1947; 85 pp. Articles which illustrate by concrete examples the methodology of Marx and Lenin.

5. *Reason and Liberty* 理 性 與 自 由 , **29**, 1946; 190 pp. A collection of articles criticizing Fung Yu-lan, Ho Lin, and Ch'ien Mu.

Chang Ju-hsin, *General Discussion of Philosophical Currents in the Soviet Union* 蘇 聯 哲 學 潮 流 概 論 , **30**, 1930; 169 pp.

2. *Dialectic and Materialism* 辯 證 法 與 唯 物 論 , **30**.

3. *Philosophy of the Proletariat* 無 產 階 級 的 哲 學 , **30**.

4. *General Discussion of Philosophy* 哲 學 概 論 , **30**, 1932. Despite its title, this is a history of philosophy having as its aim to demonstrate that dialectical materialism is the summit of human thought.

Li Chi, *Biography of Marx* 馬 克 思 傳 , **7**. In three volumes.

2. H. W. Laidler's *Socialism in Thought and Action* (translation) 社 會 主 義 之 思 想 及 運 動 , **1**.

3. *Dialectic or Pragmatism?* 辯 證 法 還 是 實 驗 主 義 , **7**.

Huang T'e, *Talks on the New Philosophy* 新 哲 學 談 話 , **31**, 1940. Another popular manual.

2. *Dialectical Materialism* 辯 證 唯 物 論 , **31**, 1940. Selections from the classics of Marxism—Marx, Engels, Lenin, etc.

3. *The Weapon of Criticism* 批 判 的 武 器 , **31**, 1941;

222 pp. A collection of critiques and expositions including criticism of Yeh Ch'ing, the philosophy of the 'New Democracy', and others.

Ch'en Wei-shih, *Popular Talks on Dialectic* 通俗辯證法講話 , 1935. Brief statement of the principal tenets of Marxism.

2. *Talks on the New Philosophical System* 新哲學体系講話 , 3², 1937; 300 pp. Refutes the non-Marxist systems and upholds neo-materialism.

3. *Talks on the Materialism of Warring Nations* 戰國唯物論講話 , 33, 1937; 265 pp. Later republished under the title *The Scientific Conception of the World of the New Philosophy*, which is more accurate.

Ko Ming-chung, *Scientific Philosophy* 科學的哲學 , 25, 1939. A more detailed treatment than most of the preceding manuals. The author seeks to prove his case by examples borrowed from biology and the other sciences.

Lin Che-jen, *Catechism on the Philosophy of the Masses* 大眾哲學問答 , 1939; 156 pp.

P'ing Sheng, *A New Philosophy Reader* 新哲學讀本 , 222 pp. Another popular manual.

Ch'en Po-ta, *The Pursuit of Truth* 真理的追求 , 1939.

2. *On T'an Ssu-t'ung* 論譚嗣同 , 34, 1934.

Wu Li-p'ing, *The Anti-Dühring of Engels* 反杜林論 , 24.

2. *Manual of the Scientific Conception of History* 科學歷史觀教程 , 1939, 271 pp. Written in collaboration with Ai Ssu-ch'i.

Chien Po-tsan, *Manual of the Philosophy of History* 歷史哲學教程, 25.

Lin Po-hsiu, Deborin's *Introduction to Dialectical Materialism* (translation) 辯證法唯物論入門 , 35.

2. Deborin's *Materialist Dialectic and the Natural Sciences* (translation) 唯物辯證法與自然科學, 30.

Chang Chung-shih, Plekhanov's *Fundamental Questions of the Social Sciences* (translation) 社會科學的基本問題 , 25, 1937, 222 pp.

2. Engels' *Origin of the Family, Property and State* (translation) 封建主義, 25.

3. Mitin's *Philosophy* (translation) 哲學, 25.

4. Rosenthal's *Knowledge According to Dialectic* (translation) 辭證認識論, 25.

Hsiang Lin-ping, *Outline of the History of Chinese Philosophy* 中國哲學史綱要, 25, 1939; 662 pp.

Kuo Mo-jo, *The Bronze Age* 青銅時代, 25, 1945; 279 pp. Essays on the religions and philosophies of antiquity.

2. *Ten Critiques* 十批判書, 36, 1945; 430 pp. Studies on ancient Chinese philosophy.

Hou Wai-lu, *History of Thought and Scholarship in Ancient China* 中國古代思想學術史, 37, 1942; 300 pp.

2. *History of Thought and Scholarship in Contemporary China* 近代中國思想學術史, 25, 1947; 600 pp. In two volumes. The author concludes that the thought of the contemporary period in China is not inferior to that of the Renaissance in Europe.

Kuo Ta-li, Marx's *Capital* (translation) 資本論, 21. Among the numerous translations of the Marxist 'Bible', this one is considered the best.

2. Lange's *History of Materialism* 唯物論史

Ho Pai-nien, J. Dietzgen's *Logic of Dialectic* (translation) 辯證法的邏輯, 35.

2. Dietzgen's *Dialectical Materialism* (translation) 辯證法唯物論, 38.

3. Marx's *Third Revolution of Napoleon* (translation) 拿破崙第三政變記, 25.

Tu Wei-chih, Engels' *Dialectic of Nature* (translation) 自然辯證法, 7.

2. Plekhanov's *Militant Materialism* 戰鬥的唯物論 7.

Ma Che-min, *General Discussion of Spirit and Science* 精神科學概論, 39, 1930; 336 pp. A study of life and the productions of the spirit from the Marxist point of view. The author is especially a student of Marxist economics.

Fu Tzu-tung, Lenin's *Materialism and Empirical Criticism* 唯 物 論 兩 經 驗 批 評 論, 7.

'MECHANISTIC' MATERIALISM

Yeh Ch'ing, *Whither Philosophy?* 哲 學 到 何 處 去, 40, 1934. Tries to prove that philosophy will become merely the 'theory of science', and hence will lose its name.

2. *Problems of Logic* 論 理 學 問 題, 40, 1935.

3. *Philosophical Controversies* 哲 學 論 戰, 40, 1935. A symposium consisting mainly of attacks of the dialectical materialists against the idealists.

4. *Problems of Philosophy* 哲 學 問 題, 40, 1936. Continuation from a different viewpoint of the argument that philosophy in the future will be merely the science of thought.

5. *The Controversies of the New Philosophy* 新 哲 學 論 戰 集, 40, 1936. Collection of the author's disputations with the 'orthodox' Marxists who accused him of betraying Marx.

6. *Struggles in the Developing of the New Philosophy* 為 發 展 新 哲 學 而 戰, 40, 1937. A continuation of the preceding.

Yang Po-k'ai, *Anthology on Philosophical Thought* 哲 學 思 想 集, 40. After Solovine's translation of Heraclitus.

2. *Anthology on Philosophy and Ethics* 哲 學 道 德 集, 40. After Solovine's translation of Democritus.

3. *Theories and Maxims* 學 說 與 格 言, 40. Theories and maxims of Epicurus.

4. d'Helvetius' *On Spirit* (translation) 精 神 論, 40.

5. Diderot's *Principles of Philosophy* (translation) 哲 學 原 理, 40.

6. Lafargue's *Origin and Evolution of Wealth* (translation) 財 產 之 起 源 與 進 化, 40.

7. Bukharin's *World Economy and Imperialism* (translation) 世 界 經 濟 與 帝 國 主 義, 40.

Wang T'e-fu, *What Is Matter?* 甚麼叫物質, 40, 1932.
2. *Theory of the Formation of the World* 世界生成論, 40.
3. *General Discussion of Physics* 物理學概論, 40.
4. *System of Logic* 論理學體系, 40.
Chang I-hung, *What Is Philosophy?* 甚麼叫做哲學, 40.
2. *General Discussion of Philosophy* 哲學概論, 40, 1936.
Jen Po-ko, La Mettrie's *Man A Machine* (translation) 人－機器, 40.
2. Stoljarov's *Critique of Mechanism* (translation) 機械論批判, 40, 1935.
T'an Fu-chih, Eddington's *Nature of the Physical World* (translation) 物質世界之本質.
2. Jeans' *New Foundation of the Sciences* (translation) 科學底基礎.
3. Pearson's *Grammar of Science* (translation) 科學規範.
4. T. H. Huxley's *Method and Results* (translation) 方法與結果.
5. *Philosophical Critiques* 哲學批判集, 1937. Critiques of Yeh Ch'ing, Ai Ssu-ch'i, vitalism, and Buddhism.

THE VOLUNTARISM OF SCHOPENHAUER AND NIETZSCHE

Wang Kuo-wei, *Ching-an Anthology* 靜菴文集, 1906.
Ching-an is another name of Wang Kuo-wei.
2. *Kuan-t'ang Anthology* 觀堂集林, 1923. Kuan-t'ang is still another name of Wang Kuo-wei.
Li Shih-ts'en, *Philosophy of the Superman* 超人哲學學說, 1. Exposition of Nietzsche's philosophy.
2. *Anthology of Li Shih-ts'en's Essays* 李石岑論文集, 1, 1924; 220 pp. Critiques of Nietzsche, Bergson, Eucken, and others.
3. *Anthology of Li Shih-ts'en's Lectures* 李石岑演講集, 1, 1924; 200 pp. Critiques of Liang Shu-ming, Russell, Dewey and Nietzsche.
4. *Philosophy of Life* 人生哲學, 1, 1926; 270 pp.

Compares solutions to the problems of life as given by various Occidental and Oriental philosophers, and then sets forth his own, which are tinged with Confucianism.

5. *Principles of Philosophy* 哲 學 大 綱, 4, 1933; 400 pp. Passes in review all the modern systems, and concludes in favour of dialectical materialism; the final stage in the evolution of his thought.

6. *Ten Lectures on Chinese Philosophy* 中 國 哲 學 十 講, 4; 454 pp. A brief history of Chinese philosophy.

Hsiao Kan, Schopenhauer's *Theory of Pessimism* (translation) 悲 觀 論 集, I.

Fang Tung-mei, *Science, Philosophy, and Life* 科 學 哲 學 與 人 生. The author is profoundly under the influence of Neitzsche as regards 'life', and 'culture', but not as regards 'voluntarism'.

PHILOSOPHICAL ANARCHISM

Wu Chih-hui, an unfinished translation of Kropotkin's *Mutual Aid*, published in a review founded in Paris about 1905, by the author and several other Chinese students. (See the present work, Part I, Section on 'The Anarchism of Kropotkin'.)

Chou Fo-hai, Kropotkin's *Mutual Aid* (translation) 互 助 論, I.

Ch'ü Jen-hsia, *Studies in Anarchism* 無 政 府 主 義 研 究.

Liu Hsü, *The Free Society* 自 由 社 會 學, 10.

Pa Chin, Kropotkin's *Origin and Development of Morals* (translation) 倫 理 學 的 起 源 和 發 展, 41.

2. Kropotkin's *Bread and Freedom* (translation) 麵 包 與 自 由, 41.

3. Kropotkin's *My Life* 我 的 自 傳, 41.

Pi Hsiu-shuo, Kropotkin's *Words of a Rebel* (translation) 一 個 反 抗 者 的 話. The author is a follower of Pa Chin.

P'u Ying, Bakhunin's *God and the State* (translation) 上 帝 與 國 家, 41.

GERMAN RATIONALISM: KANT AND HEGEL

Cheng Hsin, *Description of Kantism* 康德學述 , 1.

Nan Shu-hsi, *Kant* 康德., 4, 1934; 104 pp.

Fan Shou-k'ang, *Kant* 康德 , 1.

Hu Jen-yüan, Kant's *Critique of Pure Reason* (translation) 純粹理性批判, 1.

Chou Hsien, Kant's *Power of the Spirit* 康德的人心能力論 , 1.

Chang Tung-sun, *Philosophy* 哲學 , 4, 1931; 307 pp. Defines philosophy, and then describes its history in the Occident. Gives special attention to Kant.

2. *Modern Philosophy* 現代哲學 , 4, 1934; 108 pp. Describes pragmatism, Bergsonism, neo-idealism, neo-realism, etc. Concludes that materialism is bankrupt.

3. *New Philosophical Theories* 新哲學論叢 , 1, 1929; 466 pp. The author's own conception of the world and of life. Also criticizes pragmatism, neo-realism, relativism, and other modern currents, especially those in America.

4. *Philosophy of Value* 價值哲學, 4. The philosophical theory of the Vienna school, grafted on to Freudism.

5. *Psychoanalysis* 精神分析, 4. Popularization of Freudian theory

6. *Moral Philosophy* 道德哲學 , 2, 1930; 646 pp. Moral theories of the Occident from ancient times to the present. The author adopts a personal view closely agreeing with that of Wundt.

7. *Epistemology* 認識論 , 4, 1934. Exposition of the author's own system, termed 'the pluralism of knowledge', which derives from Kant but revises some of Kant's theories.

8. *Knowledge and Culture* 知識與文化 , 1, 1946; 237 pp. Here the author has abandoned Kant and comes at the problem of knowledge from the sociological point of view.

9. *Thought and Democracy* 思想與社會 , 1, 1946; 204 pp. Shows the influence of society on theoretical thinking.

10. *Reason and Democracy* 理 性 與 民 主 , 1, 1946; 190 pp. Shows that democracy is not merely a political system, but implies a whole civilization.

11. *Democracy and Socialism* 民 主 主 義 與 社 會 主 義 , 42, 1947; 97 pp. With this work the author has definitely abandoned metaphysics for sociology. He leans toward anarchism, but retains his moral convictions.

Ho Lin, *Brief Explanation of Contemporary Idealism* 近 代 唯 心 論 簡 釋 , 43, 1942. Analysis of current idealistic philosophies. The author believes Confucian idealism to be the most superior.

2. Royce's *Description of Hegel's Theories* (translation) 黑 格 爾 學 述 , 1.

3. Caird's *Hegel* (translation) 黑 格 爾 , 1, 1936; 224 pp.

Chang Ming-ting, Kant's *Critique of Practical Reason* (translation) 實 踐 理 性 批 判 , 1.

2. Hegel's *Logic* (translation) 黑 格 爾 論 理 學 , 4.

Shih Yu-chung, *On Mind* 談 心 , Ginling College, 1934. A sort of preface to metaphysics. Said to be profoundly influenced by Hegelianism.

2. Montague's *Methodology of Epistemology* (translation) 認 識 之 方 法 , 1.

3. *Problems of Philosophy Simply Presented* 哲 學 問 題 淺 說

Yeh Ch'ing, *Hegel* 黑 格 爾 , 40, 1935; 635 pp. Essays in honour of the centenary of Hegel by Ho Lin, Shen Chih-yüan, Chang Chün-mai, P'eng Chi-hsiang, etc.

Chu Ch'ien-chih, *Hegel and Comtism* 黑 格 爾 與 孔 德 主 義 , 44.

2. *Hegel's Philosophy of History* 黑 格 爾 的 歷 史 哲 學 , 1.

3. *A Sentimentalist's View of the Universe and Human Life* 一 個 唯 情 論 者 的 宇 宙 觀 及 人 生 觀 , 45, 1924; 178 pp. Derives from both Oriental and Occidental idealistic thought.

Kuo Pen-tao, *Hegel* 黑格爾, 4.

Shen Chih-yüan, *Hegel and Dialectic* 黑格爾與辯證法, 24. The author is a Marxist.

VARIOUS IDEALISMS: ANGLO-AMERICAN, FRENCH, ETC.

Fu T'ung-hsien, Hoernle's *Idealism as a Philosophy* (translation) 唯心哲學, 2.

2. *The Scientific Foundations of Modern Philosophy* 現代哲學之科學基礎, 1.

3. *Epistemological Theories Summarized* 知識論綱要, published by the author, 1933; 282 pp. A survey of the modern theories.

4. *Philosophy and Life* 哲學與人生, 4, 1947; 283 pp. Examines the basic problems of life—suffering, the riddle of death, good and evil, love, and religion.

Hsieh Yu-wei, *Critiques of Famous Contemporary Philosophical Works* 現代哲學名著述評, 3, 1947; 258 pp. Critical accounts of writings by Ho Lin, Hsiung Shih-li, Dewey, Whitehead, Croce, Tagore, etc.

2. *Principles of Ethics* 倫理學大綱, 3.

3. *Philosophy and Psychology* 哲理與心理, 3.

Ch'en K'ang, Plato's *Parmenides* (translation) 柏拉圖巴曼尼得斯篇, 1. The author claims to have read all of Plato in the original Greek.

Fan Shou-k'ang, *Plato* 柏拉圖, 1.

2. *Aristotle* 亞里斯多德, 1.

Kuan Ch'i-t'ung, Berkeley's *Three Dialogues* (translation) 巴克萊哲學談話三篇, 1.

2. Berkeley's *Treatise Concerning the Principles of Human Knowledge* (translation) 人類知識原理, 1.

3. Descartes' *Principles of Philosophy* (translation) 哲學原理, 1.

4. Descartes' *Discourse on Method* (translation) 笛卡爾方法論, 1.

P'eng Chi-hsiang, Levy-Brühl's *History of Modern Philosophy in France* (translation) 法 國 哲 學 史 , I.

2. Descartes' *Discourse on Method* 方 法 論 , I.

3. *Anthology of Essays on Philosophy* 哲 學 論 文 集 , 46.

Chou Fu-ch'eng, *Principles of Philosophy* 哲 學 大 綱 , 3. The author was one of the participants in the controversy between Marxists and anti-Marxists.

Ch'ü Shih-ying, *The Development of Occidental Philosophy* 西 洋 哲 學 的 發 底 , 7.

2. Hocking's *Types of Philosophy* (translation) 哲 學 大 綱 , 7.

3. *Modern Philosophy* 現 代 哲 學 , 47.

4. Booth's *Philosophy of Eucken* (translation) 倭 伊 鏗 哲 學 , I.

5. *Metaphysics* 形 而 上 學 , 4.

6. *Evolutionist Philosophy* 進 化 哲 學 , 4.

7. *Main Currents of Modern Philosophical Thought* 現 代 哲 學 思 想 潮 綱 要 , 2.

Chang Pao-heng, *Philosophy and Contemporary Science* 哲 學 與 近 代 科 學 , 4. Defends philosophy against scientific determinism.

Chan Wen-hu, Durant's *Mansions of Philosophy* (translation) 哲 學 概 論 , 5.

2. Rogers' *History of Philosophy* (translation) 西 洋 哲 學 史 , 48.

3. Weber's *History of Philosophy* (translation) 西 洋 哲 學 史 , 4.

4. Durant's *Story of Philosophy* (translation) 哲 學 的 故 事 , 49.

Ch'ing Tse-p'eng, Cunningham's *Problems of Philosophy* (translation) 哲 學 大 綱 , 4.

2. Stoce's *Critical History of Greek Philosophy* (translation) 批 評 的 希 臘 哲 學 史 , I.

3. Wulf's *Philosophy and Civilization in the Middle Ages* (translation) 中 古 哲 學 與 文 明 , I.

Wu Kuang-chien, Merz's *History of European Thought in the Nineteenth Century* (translation) 十九世紀歐洲思想史 , 1.

2. Joad and Strachey's *After-Dinner Philosophy* 飯後哲學 , 1.

3. Hume's *Inquiry Concerning Human Understanding* (translation) 人之悟性論 , 1.

P'an Tzu-nien, Jones' *Inductive and Deductive Logic* (translation) 邏輯 , 1.

2. Bergson's *Time and Free Will* (translation) 時間與意志自由 , 1. Since publication of this book the translator, brother of a Communist official, has gone over to dialectical materialism.

Chang Tung-sun, Bergson's *Matter and Memory* (translation) 物質與記憶, 1.

2. Bergson's *Creative Evolution* (translation) 創化論 , 1.

3. Plato's *Six Dialogues* (translation) 柏拉圖對話集六種 , 1.

T'ang Ch'eng-ch'e, Salomon's *Bergson* (translation) 柏格森 , 45.

2. Carr's *Bergsonian Philosophy of Evolution* (translation) 柏格森之易變哲學 , 1.

Fei Hung-nien, *Driesch and His Theories* 杜里舒及其學說 , 1.

Chiang Shao-yüan. Driesch's *Problem of Individuality* (translation) 實生論大旨 , 20. Driesch visited China on a lecture tour in 1922.

Miao Feng-lin, *Outline of the History of Ancient and Medieval Philosophy in the Occident* 西洋古代中世哲學史大綱 , 2.

2. *Outline of the History of Modern Philosophy in the Occident* 近代西洋哲學史大綱 , 2.

P'eng Chien-min, Hoffding's *Brief History of Modern Philosophy* (translation) 西洋近世哲學史 , 44.

Ching Yu-nan, *New Treatise on Philosophy* 哲學新論 , 50.

THE SPECIALISTS IN LOGIC AND METHODOLOGY

Chin Yüeh-lin, *Logic* 邏輯 , published by Tsinghua University, 1935. Follows the principles of Russell's mathematical logic. The book is nothing but a mass of algebraic formulas, but the thought is logically sound.

2. *On the Tao* 論道 , 1, 1940. Goes on from T. H. Green's criticisms of Hume to create a new system based on several concepts of ancient Chinese thought. This work is rich in its constructive spirit.

Chang Shih-chao, Sperber's *Principles of Inflection of the Voice According to the Feelings* 情為語變之原論 , 1.

2. *Essentials of Logic* 邏輯指要 , 51 , 1943. Demonstrates that the elements to compose a Chinese 'logic' exist, but have not yet been systematically exploited.

Fan Shou-k'ang, *Epistemology* 認識論 , 1.

2. *On Logic* 論理學 , 5. The numerous writings of this author have not been mentioned in the histories of contemporary philosophy since they seem to be too superficial, too much like student's manuals.

3. *Philosophy and Its Fundamental Problems* 哲學及其根本問題 , 5. On the transcendentals—truth, goodness, and beauty. More profound than this author's other works.

Lin Chung-ta, *Elements of Logic* 論理學網要 , 2.

2. *Synthetic Logic* 綜合邏輯 , 2, 1936. Deals especially with pragmatic logic and the symbolic logic of Anglo-American neo-realism.

Wang Chang-huan, *Complete Logic* 論理學大全 , 1, 1930.

Chu Chao-ts'ui, *Logic* 論理學 , 4.

2. *The A.B.C. of Logic* 論理學 A.B.C., 4.

Ho Chao-ch'ing, *Elements of Logic* 論理學大綱 , 13. Much deeper than the two preceding.

Chiang Heng-yüan, *The Scope of Logic* 論理學大意 , 52.

Chang Hsi-chih, *Elements of Logic* 論理學網要 , 47.

Wang T'e-fu, *System of Logic* 論理學體系 , **40.** Material-istic logic, tinged with Marxism.

Hung Ch'ien, *The Philosophy of the Vienna School* 維也納學派哲學 , **1.** Exposition of theories of Moritz Schlick and Rudolf Carnap.

N.B.—For other works on logic, see under the pragmatic, Russellian, and other pertinent theories.

THE PRINCIPAL SPECIALISTS IN ETHICS AND PHILOSOPHY OF LIFE

Huang Chien-chung, *Comparative Ethics* 比較倫理學 **53**; 432 pp.

T'ang Chün-i, *Establishment of the Moral Self* 道德自我之建立 , **1**, 1944; 144 pp. Treats of the origin and practice of morals.

2. *Comparative Studies on the Philosophies and Thought of China and the Occident* 中西哲學思想之比較研究集 , **3**, 1934; 410 pp. The author seeks to establish the essential character of each civilization. He is influenced by neo-Hegelian thought.

3. *The Gospel of Love* (translation)—(Fr. Brière has not noted the author) 愛情之福音 , **3.**

Lo Chia-lun, *A New Conception of Life* 新人生觀 , **1**, 1942; 109 pp. Advocates idealism and deplores scientific mechanism.

2. *A New Conception of the Nation* 新民族觀 , **1**, 1946; 140 pp. Collection of lectures delivered at National Central University. Follows the English political theorists somewhat.

Ts'ai Yüan-p'ei, Paulsen's *System of Ethics* (translation) 倫理學原理 , **1.**

2. *History of Chinese Ethics* 中國倫理學史 , **1.**

Yü Chia-chü, *Ethics Simply Explained* 倫理學淺說 , **1.**

2. Dewey and Tufts' *Ethics* (translation) 道德學 , **2.**

3. Eucken's *Meaning and Value of Life* (translation) 人生之意義與價值 , **2.**

Hsieh Fu-ya, *Philosophy of Life* 人 生 哲 學 , 4, 1929. Advocates Christian principles, the author being a Protestant.

2. Royce's *Religious Aspect of Philosophy* (translation) 宗 教 哲 學 , 1.

3. *Ethics* 倫 理 學 , 4.

Hsieh Yu-wei, *Elements of Ethics* 倫 理 學 大 綱 , 3.

2. Royce's *Philosophy of Loyalty* (translation) 忠 之 哲 學 , 1.

3. Bradley's *Ethical Studies* (translation) 倫 理 學 研 究 , 1.

Huang Fang-kang, *Ethics* 道 德 學 , 1935. Partly based on the *a priori* categories of Kant.

2. *Socrates* 蘇 格 拉 底 , 1, 1935; 119 pp. Based on Burnet, Dickinson, and A. E. Taylor.

Wang Shao-lun, *System of Ethics* 倫 理 學 體 系 , 1, 1945; 212 pp. Treats of the origin, nature, and laws of ethics. Addressed to the youth of China who have become bewildered by the events of the political scene.

2. *Elements of a Philosophy of the Nation* 民 族 哲 學 大 綱 , 3.

3. *China's Road* 中 國 之 路 , 1, 1946.

Tu Ya-ch'üan, *Philosophy of Life* 人 生 哲 學 , 1, 1949. Holds a biological point of view and is rather positivistic.

2. *Philosophy of Being in the World* 處 世 哲 學 , 1.

Chiang Heng-yüan, *Human Nature According to Early Chinese Philosophy* 中 國 先 哲 學 人 性 論 , 1.

2. *General Discussion of Ethics* 倫 理 學 概 論 , 52.

THE SPECIALISTS IN PSYCHOLOGY AND EDUCATION

Ch'en Ta-ch'i, Marbe's *Psychology of Judgment* (translation) 審 判 心 理 學 大 意 , 1.

2. *Elements of Psychology* 心 理 學 大 綱 , 1. The author is somewhat under the influence of the Anglo-American school of neo-realism.

Kuo Jen-yüan, *The A.B.C. of Psychology* 心 理 學 A.B.C., 4.
The author is the foremost Chinese specialist on behaviourism.

2. *Exposition of Behaviourist Psychology* 行 為 主 義 心 理
學 講 義 , 1.

3. *Human Conduct* 人 類 的 行 為 , 1. From the behaviourist point of view.

4. *Foundations of Behaviourism* 行 為 學 的 基 礎 , 1.
A popularization.

5. *Psychology and Heredity* 心 理 學 與 遺 傳, 1.

Hsieh Hsün-ch'u, *Behaviourist Psychology* 行 為 心 理 學, 47.

Ch'en Te-jung, *Behaviourism* 行 為 主 義 , 1.

2. Watson's *Behaviourism* (translation) 華 生 氏 行 為 主
義 , 1.

3. Pillsbury's *History of Psychology* (translation) 心 理 學
史 , 1.

4. Flügel's *Theories of Psychoanalysis* (translation) 解 心 術
學 說 , 1.

Kao Chüeh-fu, *Contemporary Psychology* 現 代 心 理 學 , 1.

2. Freud's *Psychoanalysis* (translation) 精 神 分 析 引 論 ,
1. With English and Chinese texts facing.

3. Freud's *New Introductory Lectures to Psychoanalysis* (translation)
精 神 分 析 引 論 新 篇

4. Koffka and Köhler's *One Aspect of Gestalt Psychology* (translation) 格 式 心 理 學 之 片 面 觀 , 1.

Hsiao Hsiao-jung, Koffka's *Principles of Gestalt Psychology* 格 式
心 理 學 原 理, 1.

2. *Educational Psychology* 教 育 心 理 學 , 3.

3. *Abnormal Psychology* 變 態 心 理 學 , 3.

Chu Kuang-ch'ien, *Abnormal Psychology* 變 態 心 理 學
, 1.

Kuo I-ts'en, Pavlov and Schniermann's *Psychological Studies in Russia*
(translation) 蘇 俄 新 興 心 理 學 , 2.

Shu Hsin-ch'eng, *First Steps in Psychology* 心 理 學 初 步 ,
2.

2. Moore's *Foundations of Psychology* 現代心理學之趨勢 , 2.

3. *Philosophy of Life* 人生哲學 , 2, 1923. Distinctly positivistic.

4. *Thorough Treatise on Education* 教育通論 , 2. In this field the author is the foremost specialist in China, and has written numerous studies. He was for a long time director of the great Chung Hua Book Company.

Yü Chia-chü, *Principles of Education* 教育原理 , 2.

2. Finney's *Social Philosophy of Education* (translation) 教育社會哲學 , 2.

3. *Essentials of Chinese Educational History* 中國教育史要 , 2.

Chao Yen, Allport's *Social Psychology* (translation) 社會心理學 , 1.

2. Thorndyke's *Human Learning* (translation) 人類的學習 , 1.

3. *The Psychology and Education of Talent* 天才心理與教育 , 1.

4. Low's *Theory of Psychoanalysis* (translation) 弗洛物心理分析 , 1.

Chu Chün-i, *Outline of Educational Psychology* 教育心理學大綱 , 2.

2. Garrett's *Statistics in Psychology and Education* (translation) 心理與教育之統計法 , 1.

Ai Wei, *Psychology of Elementary Education* 初級教育心理學 , 1. In several volumes.

Liao Shih-ch'eng, *Educational Psychology* 教育心理學 , 2.

2. Colvin and Bagley's *Human Behaviour* (translation) 教育心理學大意 .

Lu Chih-wei, *Psychology of Thought* 思想的心理學 , 4.

2. *Psychology* 心理學 , 1.

3. Binet and Simon's *Measurement of Intelligence* (translation)

兒童心智發達測量法, 1. This book has been translated into Chinese at least three times.

Chang Kung-piao, Le Bon's *Psychological Laws of the Evolution of Peoples* (translation) 民族進化的理定律, 1.

P'an Tzu-nien, Woodworth's *Dynamic Psychology* (translation) 動的心理學, 1.

2. Hart's *Psychology of Insanity* 瘋狂心理, 46.

Chiang Ch'i, *History of Education* 教育史, 1. Textbook for normal schools.

2. *Outline of the History of Education in the Occident* 西洋教育史大綱, 1.

Fan Ch'i, *Philosophy of Education* 教育哲學, 4.

2. *Latest Currents of Educational Thought in Europe and America* 最近歐美教育思潮, 5.

3. *General Discussion of Philosophy* 哲學概論, 1.

THE STUDIES ON AESTHETICS

Ts'ai Yüan-p'ei, *Outline of Philosophy* 哲學綱要, 1, 1924; 142 pp. The author proposes the replacement of religion by art. He is influenced especially by Windelband.

Chu Kuang-ch'ien, *Critique of the Philosophy of Croce* 克羅齊哲學評述, 3, 1948; 114 pp.

2. Croce's *Aesthetics* (translation) 美學原理, 3. This book exists in Chinese translation by another recognized scholar, Fu Tung-hua, according to the catalogue of the Commercial Press.

3. *On Beauty* 談美, 5, 1932; 137 pp. A popularization for young people of the author's views.

4. *Psychology of Literary Art* 文藝心理學, 54, 1936; 339 pp. Creation and aesthetic play. Stresses Croce's views, but also takes cognizance of Kant, Hegel, Guyau, *et al.*

5. *On Poetry* 詩論, 3, 1948; 242 pp. Another successful work by this author, whose books are well thought out and well written. He preaches 'making life an art'.

T'ung-hsien, *Outline of Aesthetics* 美 學 綱要 , 2, 1948;
Fu138 pp. Stresses Croce, Santayana and Dewey.

Feng Tzu-k'ai *Artistic Taste* 藝 術 趣 味 , 5. The author's
own talent in art lies in cartooning, but he devotes his attention
in this and other writings especially to the beauties of music.

Chin Kung-liang, *Principles of Aesthetics* 美 學 原 理, 3, 1936;
114 pp. An adaptation of Roger's *Beauty*. The adaptor teaches at
the school of fine arts in Hangchow.

Li An-chai, *Aesthetics* 美 學 , 4. This author has also done a
translation of Frazer's *Sympathetic Magic*.

Fan Shou-k'ang, *General Discussion of Aesthetics* 美 學 概 論, 1.

Ch'en Wang-tao, *General Discussion of Aesthetics* 美 學 概
論 , 44.

Hsü Ch'ing-yü, *Philosophy of Beauty* 美 的 哲 學 , published
by the author, 1928. The author, a Protestant, refutes the thesis of
Ts'ai Yüan-p'ei, and establishes that art cannot replace religion.

Hu Ch'iu-yüan, Friche's *Sociology of Art* (translation) 藝 術 社
會 學 , 7. This book had already been translated four times
before 1935, and has just been published in still another translation.

Kuo Mo-jo, Michaelis' *History of Archeological Discoveries in the Fine
Arts* (translation) 美 術 考 古 一 世 紀, 36. An old
work, recently republished.

Ts'ai I, *The New Aesthetics* 新美 學 , 36, 1948; 285 pp. The
first of a series of books designed to explain aesthetics from the
Marxist point of view. It essays to refute the theories of Kant,
Croce, and their interpreter, Chu Kuang-ch'ien.

2. Friche's *Artistic Sociology* (translation) 藝 術 社會學 ,
36.

Hu Man, *History of the Fine Arts in China* 中 國美術史 ,
36, 1946; 216 pp. 'Art was formerly based on oppression of the
people; it must be returned to the people', says the preface.

Ch'en Yüan, Tschaikovsky's *My Life in Music* (translation) 我 的
音樂 生 活, 36.

Su Ch'iao, Albred's *Life of Picasso* (translation) 俾卡索傳 ,
36.

2. Symonds' *Life of Michelangelo* (translation) 米啟蘭琪羅傳 , 36.

Shen Ch'i-yü, Taine's *Philosophy of Art* (translation) 藝術哲學 , 36. In course of translation.

Lei Jan, Stanislavsky's *My Life in Art* (translation) 我的藝術生活 , 36. Like all the above-listed works published by this company, this is in the Marxist series of studies.

Ch'en Chu-shan, *The Art of Living* 人生藝術 , 1, 1944; 240 pp. A theory of morals based on aesthetics; beauty is the supreme value of life.

2. *The Cradle of Philosophy* 哲學之故鄉 , 2. A history of classical Greek philosophy.

Lü Ch'eng, *General Discussion of Aesthetics* 美學概論 , 1.

2. *Currents of Modern Aesthetic Thought* 現代美學思潮 , 1.

3. *Theory of Colour* 色彩學 , 1.

Teng I-chih, *Difficulties of Artists* 藝術家的難關 .

Tsung Pai-hua, *Concerning the Meaning of Art* 對於藝術的意境 .

Wu Mi, 'Artistic Cultivation and the Religious Spirit' 藝術修養與宗教精神 . An article in the review *Building the Nation* 建國導報 , no. 1.

2. Hoernle's *God, Soul. Life, Matter* (translation) 神、心靈、生命、物質 .

Feng Chih, Schiller's *On Aesthetic Education* (translation) 論美育 .

2. *Fourteen Poems* 十四行詩集 .

N.B.—The reader will perhaps be surprised not to find any mention of the efforts made by the Catholics to introduce philosophy of Catholic derivation. It must be confessed that apart from the manuals for seminaries the pickings are very slim. We can cite among recent works the *Introduction to Philosophy* by Maritain, translated by Tai Ming-wo. The *Summa* of St. Thomas is now in course of reprinting after a new translation. In a broad sense, certain general syntheses are of more or less Catholic derivation, such as the translations of Dawson's *Progress and Religion*, Carrell's *Man the*

Unknown, du Noüy's *Human Destiny*, Gilson's *Modern Thought and Catholicism*, etc. And finally, we can mention the *Epistemology* 認識論 of P. Czech, S.V.D., published by the Commercial Press in 1948, a deep work by a professor of Fujen University (Peiping), as well as the works of Fr. R. Vinciarelli, O.S.B.

PUBLISHERS

Note: In order to avoid excessive use of Chinese characters in the text of the Bibliography, the translator has brought together all publishers (most of which are in Shanghai) in the following list. The publisher of any particular work in the Bibliography may be identified by the number printed in bold-faced type, according to this list. (In some cases publisher and/or date was not given by author.)

1. Commercial Press 商務印書館
2. Chung Hua Book Company 中華書局
3. Cheng Chung Book Company 正中書局
4. Shih Chieh (World) Book Company 世界書局
5. K'ai Ming Book-store 開明書店
6. Fo Hsüeh (Buddhist) Book Company 佛學書局
7. Shen Chou Book-store 社州書店
8. Wen Jen Book-store 文人書店
9. Sheng Li Publishers 勝利出版
10. Ch'ün Chung Book-store 群眾書店
11. Hsiang Ts'un Book-store 鄉邨書店
12. Ya Tung Book Company 亞東書局
13. Chung Shan Book Company 鍾山書局
14. Ch'ing Nien Book-store 青年書店
15. I Hsüeh (Medical) Book Company 醫學書局
16. Pa T'i Book-store 拔堤書店
17. Anhwei Fan Sheng Yüan 安徽反省院
18. Tso Che Book-store 作者書店
19. Hsin Yüeh Book-store 新月書店
20. Ya Tung Library 亞東圖書館

21. Tu Shu Sheng Huo Publishers 讀書生活出版
22. Ch'en Kuang Book-store 辰光書店
23. K'un Lun Book Company 崑崙書局
24. Pi Keng Hall 筆耕堂
25. Sheng Huo Book-store 生活書店
26. Hsin Chih Book-store 新知書店
27. Hsin Hua Book-store 新華書店
28. Keng Yün Publishing Company 耕耘出版社
29. Hua Hsia Book-store 華夏書店
30. Kuang Hua Book-store 光華書店
31. Hsin Jen Publishers 新人出版
32. *Shanghai Magazine* 上海雜志
33. Tso Chia Book-store 作家書店
34. *Ta Kung Pao* (a newspaper) 大公報
35. Nan Ch'iang Book Company 南強書局
36. Ch'ün I Publishing Company 群益出版社
37. Wen Feng Book-store 文風書店
38. Hsien Tai Book Company 現代書局
39. Hsin Sheng Ming Book Company 新生命書局
40. Hsin K'en Book-store 辛墾書局
41. Wen Hua Sheng Huo Publishing Company 文化生活出版社
42. Kuan Ch'a Company 觀察社
43. Tu Li Publishing Company 獨立出版社
44. Min Chih Book Company 民智書局
45. T'ai Tung Library 泰東圖書館
46. Pei Hsin Book Company 北新書局
47. Wen Hua Company 文化社
48. Hsin Chung Kuo Book-store 新中國書店
49. Ch'ing Hsieh Book-store 青協書店
50. Nanking ?Book Company 南京 ? [書局]
51. Shih Tai Ching Shen Publishing Company 時代精神出版社
52. Ta Tung Book Company 大東書局
53. Chung Kuo Wen Hua Fu Wu Company 中國文化服務社
54. Peiping Book-store 北平書店
55. Ch'ün Hsüeh Company 群學社

BIBLIOGRAPHY
OF WRITINGS IN WESTERN LANGUAGES
ON CONTEMPORARY CHINESE THOUGHT
(Appended by the Translator)

---

1. Brière, O., S.J., 'L'Effort de la philosophie marxiste en Chine', *Bulletin de l'Université l'Aurore*, Shanghai, série III, tome 8, no. 3 (complete series no. 31), 1947; pp. 309–47. With bibliography. A fuller treatment of Marxism in China than that given in the present work.

   Fr. Brière has done additional articles on subjects closely related to the general theme of contemporary Chinese thought, which have been published in *B.U.A.* The most important of these is 'Les tendances dominantes de la littérature chinoise contemporaine', in série III, tome 9 (complete series no. 35), 1948; pp. 234–69—an article covering the period 1917–48.

2. Carus, Paul, 'Ceremony Celebrated under the Chinese Republic in Honour of Confucius', *Open Court*, vol. XXXII, March 1918; pp. 55–72.

3. Chan, Wing-tsit, 'Trends in Contemporary Philosophy', being chapter 20 of *China*, H. F. MacNair, editor, Berkeley and Los Angeles, University of California Press, 1946; pp. 312–30. This is a slightly revised version of the author's 'Philosophies of China', in *Twentieth Century Philosophy*, Dagobert D. Runes, editor, New York, Philosophical Library, 1943; pp. 541–71.

4. Chang Tung-sun, 'A Chinese Philosopher's Theory of Knowledge' (his own). Translated from the Chinese by Li An-che from an article entitled 'Thought, Language and Culture,' in *Sociological World*, vol. X, June 1938. Li's translation appeared in *The Yenching Journal of Social Studies*, vol. I, no. 2, January 1939; pp. 155–91.

5. Ch'en Li-fu, *Philosophy of Life*, translated from the Chinese by Jen Tai. New York, Philosophical Library, 1948; 148 pp.

6. Doré, Henri, 'Le Confucéisme sous la République, 1911–1922', *New China Review*, vol. IV, 1922; pp. 298–319.

7. Dubs, Homer H., 'Recent Chinese Philosophy', *Journal of Philosophy*, vol. XXXV, no. 13, 1938; pp. 345–55.

8. Elia, Paschal M. d', S.J., *The Triple Demism of Sun Yat-sen*. Translated from the French original entitled *Le Triple Demisme de Suen Wen*, Shanghai, 1930. Wuchang, The Franciscan Press, 1931. The English translation is stated by the author himself to be a better work than the original. See also 31 below.

9. Forke, Alfred, *Geschichte der Neueren Chinesischen Philosophie*, Hamburg, 1938; 693 pp. Pages 571–650 deal with nineteenth- and twentieth-century philosophers.

10. Forster, Lancelot, *The New Culture in China*, London, 1936.

11. ——, 'Revival of Confucianism', *Asia Magazine*, vol. XXXV, September 1935; pp. 527–30. Illustrated.

12. Franke, Wolfgang, 'Die Staatspolitischen Reformversuche K'ang Yu-weis und seiner Schule. Ein Beitrag zur gestigen Auseinandersetzung Chinas mit dem Abendlande', *Mitteilungen des Seminars für Orientalische Sprachen an der Friedrich-Wilhelms-Universität zu Berlin*, Jahrgang XXXVIII, erste Abteilung: Ostasiatische Studien. Berlin, 1935; pp. 1–83.

13. Fung Yu-lan, *A Comparative Study of Life Ideals*, Shanghai, 1924.

14. ——, *A History of Chinese Philosophy*. Translated by Derk Bodde. In two volumes. The first was published by Henri Vetch, Peiping, in 1937, and republished by Princeton University Press in 1952, with corrections and additions. The second volume was published by Princeton University Press in 1953: London, George Allen and Unwin, 1954.

15. ——, 'Philosophy in Contemporary China', in *Supplement to a History of Chinese Philosophy* 中國哲學史補, Shanghai, Commercial Press, 1936. While the book is written in Chinese, this special article is in English.

16. Fung Yu-lan, *A Short History of Chinese Philosophy*. Edited by Derk Bodde. New York, The MacMillan Company, 1948. See chapters 27 and 28, pp. 319–42.

17. ———, *The Spirit of Chinese Philosophy*. Translated from the Chinese by E. R. Hughes. The English title is actually the subtitle of the original work, which is called the *New Treatise on the Nature of Tao* 新原道 , Shanghai, Commercial Press, 1945. Described by the author as a supplement to his two-volume *History of Chinese Philosophy* (14 above). London, Routledge & Kegan Paul, 1947.

18. Han Yü-shan, 'Some Tendencies of Contemporary Chinese Philosophy', *Journal of Philosophy*, vol. xxv, no. 19, 1928; pp. 505–13.

19. Hu Shih, *The Chinese Renaissance*, Chicago, University of Chicago Press, 1934.

20. ———, 'Intellectual China in 1919', *The Chinese Social and Political Science Review*, vol. iv, no. 4, December 1919; pp. 345–55.

21. ———, 'The Literary Revolution in China', *ibid.*, vol. vi, no. 2, 192(1?); pp. 91–100.

22. Hughes, E. R., *The Invasion of China by the Western World*, London, Adam & Charles Black, 1937; 324 pp. With bibliography. To date this is the best rounded work attempting to cover this broad and important subject. It is doubly valuable because it is written largely from Chinese sources.

23. Hummel, Arthur W., translator and editor, *The Autobiography of a Chinese Historian, Being the Preface to a Symposium on Ancient Chinese History* (*Ku Shih Pien*), Leiden, E. J. Brill, 1931. The Chinese historian is Ku Chieh-kang, one of the most eminent scholars of contemporary China. This work throws light on contemporary intellectual matters in general.

24. Kiang Wen-han, *The Chinese Student Movement*, New York, 1948.

25. Latourette, Kenneth Scott, *The Chinese, Their History and Culture*, New York, The MacMillan Company, 1934. Revised

editions, 1943 and 1946. Two Volumes (in one). See vol. I, chapter 12; vol. II, chapters 16 and 19.

26. Lin Mousheng, *Men and Ideas, An Informal History of Chinese Political Thought*, New York, The John Day Company, 1942. See chapter 15 on K'ang Yu-wei.

27. Millican, Frank R., 'Philosophical and Religious Thought in China', *China Christian Year Book*, Shanghai, 1926; pp. 423–69. An important article.

28. Reinsch, Paul S., *Intellectual and Political Currents in the Far East*, Boston and New York, 1911. See especially chapter 4, 'Intellectual Tendencies in the Chinese Reform Movement'.

29. Schwartz, Benjamin, *Chinese Communism and the Rise of Mao*, Cambridge, Harvard University Press, 1951. Chapter 1, 'The Origin of Marxism-Leninism in China', discusses Ch'en Tu-hsiu and Li Ta-chao.

30. Shen, Nelson Nai-cheng, 'The Changing Chinese Social Mind', *The Chinese Social and Political Science Review*, Part One, in vol. VIII, no. 1, January 1924; Part Two, in vol. VIII, no. 2, April 1924.

31. Sun Yat-sen (Sun Wen), *San Min Chu I, The Three Principles of the People*. Translated from the Chinese by Frank Price. Shanghai, 1928. See also 8 above.
   N.B.—This bibliography does not include the numerous works relating to Dr. Sun or the Chinese revolutionary movement. Such works lie outside of the present field of interest, even though they are obviously pertinent to it.

32. Teng Ssu-yü, John K. Fairbank, and Sun E-tu Zen, *China's Response to the West, A Documentary Survey (1839–1923)*, Harvard University Press, 1954.

33. Ts'ai Yüan-p'ei, 'Tendencies toward Harmony between Eastern and Western Political Ideas', *The Chinese Social and Political Science Review*, vol. II, no. 1, March 1918; pp. 41–9. Translated from the Chinese by L. K. Tao.

34. Tseng Yu-hao, *Modern Chinese Legal and Political Philosophy*, Shanghai, Commercial Press, 1934; 320 pp.

35. Tsuchida Kyoson, *Contemporary Thought of Japan and China*, London, Williams & Norgate, 1927. On Chinese thought see chapters 10 and 11. Brief but informative.

36. Vargas, P. de, 'Some Elements in the Chinese Renaissance', *New China Review*, vol. IV, 1922; pp. 115–27 and 234–47.

37. Wang Ching-tao, *Confucius and New China*, Shanghai, d.?

38. Wieger, Léon, *La Chine Moderne. Mouvement d'émancipation et de modernisation*, Hien-hien, 10 vols., 1921–32. The first two of these volumes, *Prodromes* (1931) and *Le Flot Montant* (1921) are cited in the present work.

39. Wilhelm, Richard, 'Intellectual Movements in Modern China', *The Chinese Social and Political Science Review*, vol. VIII, no. 2, April 1924; pp. 110–24.

40. ——, *The Soul of China*. Translated from the German by John Holroyd Reece. New York, Harcourt, Brace & Company, 1928. Experiences, observations, and reflections of a sensitive Western scholar long resident in China, much of whose interest lay in the field of Chinese thought.

41. Levenson, J. R., '"History" and "Value": the Tensions of Intellectual Thought in Modern China'. Being an essay in *Studies in Chinese Thought*, Arthur F. Wright, editor, Chicago, University of Chicago Press, 1953; pp. 146–94.

42. ——, *Liang Ch'i-ch'ao and the Mind of Modern China*, Cambridge (Mass.), Harvard University Press, 1953.

43. Chan, Wing-tsit, *Religious Trends in Modern China*, New York, Columbia University Press, 1953.

44. Hunter, Edward, *Brain-Washing in Red China*, New York, Vanguard Press. First published 1951, enlarged edition 1953. Enlightening as to what sort of philosophical activity may be expected under Communist control, and as to the kind of pressures which have led such philosophers as Fung Yu-lan to 'recant'.

INDEX OF CHINESE PERSONS

INDEX

153

LIANG Jen-kung (*see* LIANG Ch'i-ch'ao) 任公
LIAO Shih-ch'eng 廖世承, 138
LIN Che-jen 林哲人, 124
LIN Chung-ta 林仲達, 8, 134
LIN Po-hsiu 林伯修, 124
LIN Yutang 林語堂, 1895– , 93, 95, 102n.
LIU Ch'i-wei 柳其偉, 121
LIU Hsü 柳絮, 128
LIU Po-ming 劉伯明, 120
LO Chia-lun 羅家倫, 1895– , 8, 93, 102n., 135
LU Chih-wei 陸志韋, 138f.
LÜ Ch'eng 呂澂, 117, 141

MA Che-min 馬哲民, 125
MA Chün-wu 馬君武, 1881–1940, 20
MA I-fu 馬一浮, 1882– , 56f., 71
MAO Tse-tung 毛澤東, 1893– , 35, 80, 81
MENCIUS (MENG TZU 孟子), ? 372–? 289 B.C., 29, 56, 60, 114
MENG Hsien-ch'eng 孟憲承, 121
MIAO Feng-lin 繆鳳林, 133
MO Ti 墨翟, *c.* 479–*c.* 381 B.C., 25, 63, 89, 114, 115
MOU Tsung-san 牟宗三, 1908– , 72

NAN Shu-hsi 南庶熙, 129

OU-YANG Chien (*see* OU-YANG Ching-wu) 漸
OU-YANG Ching-wu 歐陽竟無, 1871–1943, 40, 42, 117

PA Chin 巴金, 1905– , 21, 22, 128
P'AN Tzu-nien 潘梓年, 133, 139
P'ENG Chi-hsiang 彭基相, 130, 131
P'ENG Chien-min 彭健民, 133
PI Hsiu-shuo 畢修勺, 128
P'ING Sheng 平生, 124
P'U Ying 朴英, 128

SHEN Ch'i-yü 沈起予, 141
SHEN Chih-yüan 沈志遠, 1902– , 79f., 90, 122, 130
SHIH Yu-chung 施友忠, 1902– , 72f., 130

INDEX OF NON-CHINESE PERSONS